Out of the Shadows

D1501229

Out of the Shadows

Stories of Adoption and Reunion

Linda Back McKay

NORTH STAR PRESS OF ST. CLOUD, INC.

Saint Cloud, Minnesota

Cover design by Judith Connor

Copyright (c) 2012 Linda Back McKay

ISBN 978-0-87839-623-8

First Edition: September 2012

Printed in the United States of America

Published by
North Star Press of St. Cloud, Inc.
P.O. Box 451
St. Cloud, Minnesota 56302

www.northstarpress.com   Facebook - North Star Press

Dedication

For the light in my life—
Allie, Nick, Evan, Gabriel, Mikayla and Atari

And, for those who still cower in shadows.

Acknowledgements

Heartfelt thanks to Barbara Leigh Kaplan, who embarked on the original *Shadow Mothers* journey with me, those many years ago. Judith Connor, thank you for your steadfast friendship and artistry.

Thanks also to the women featured here—for their great courage and generosity in sharing their stories and insights. Peace and love to each of you. And to Lily Baber Coyle, Ron Peluso, and the History Theatre for getting it right.

A loving thank you to my family and friends for your ongoing support.

And thanks to the editors and publishers of the following magazines and books, in which some of the author's poems first appeared: *Lipservice, Minnesota Monthly, Parting Gifts, the Antigonish Review, Ride That Full Tilt Boogie* (2001 North Star Press) and *The Next Best Thing* (2011 Nodin Press).

The song lyrics contained in Jan's story are the property of Jan Seides-Murphy, all rights reserved.

Table of Contents

A Note from the Author

WHAT AN INCREDIBLE RIDE IT'S BEEN. Since *Shadow Mothers* was first published in 1998, I have learned so much—what it's like to be public with my story and my life, how to handle other people's responses, the fun and not-so-fun things authors need to do to market their books, how an author is seen as an authority on her subject matter, how to deal with failure and success, how to sell books out of the trunk of one's car or the saddlebags of one's motorcycle, and more.

During the first years after publication, I gave readings at bookstores and book clubs in various parts of the country. I participated in adoption-related panel discussions and appeared occasionally as a featured speaker or facilitator. I've hosted and monitored chat rooms and was active in a variety of support groups. I was interviewed hundreds of times on radio programs and dozens of times for newspaper and television. I have written adoption-related articles for magazines and websites.

Yes, I made the effort, but I am still amazed at how, almost immediately, *Shadow Mothers* seemed to take on its own life and move into the world to touch people in so many different ways. I believe it continues to live because it is a book that our world needs. *Shadow Mothers* was a groundbreaking book—the first that examined the experiences of "unwed mothers," along with adoption and reunion experiences from the points of view of ordinary people. I'm one of them. I am not a social worker, or any kind of counselor, although I have often found myself in a position to offer logical, common sense advice. The work I continue to do around *Shadow Mothers* is good work. I feel grateful about doing it.

Even to this day I get regular emails from people who have discovered my book and contact information. Adopted people ask me how to approach birthparents who were recently located. People ask about how to search. How to respond when one or the other party in a reunion backs away. Why a birthparent acts so damaged. How to get over the sadness. Why an adult birth child is so angry. How to understand the avalanche of emotions that comes with reunion. How to incorporate the birth or adoptive family into their families. How to move on with their lives. How to be "normal" (whatever that is). I do not tell people what to do, but I offer my opinion as a birthmother, adoptive mother and "standard" mother with a lot of research under her belt. People need to do what is right in their hearts. I have heard hundreds of reunion stories. There are as many kinds of stories as there are kinds of people. Some are heartbreaking, some are joyful, but most are a bittersweet mix.

In late 1998 I was industriously setting up radio interviews around the country and in Canada with anyone who would have me on their program. The wonderful thing about radio interviews is that they can be conducted by telephone, which is very helpful to an author without a marketing budget. I had good success with those efforts. There was much interest in the topic of unmarried mothers, probably because it had been such a hush-hush subject. Many people have been touched by adoption in some way, and adoption reunions were beginning to happen more and more often. Looking back, I believe *Shadow Mothers* was ahead of its time. I like to think that it helped to start bringing these life experiences out of the shadows and into the light of understanding.

One of the programs in which I was interviewed was "Mid-Morning." It was hosted by Katherine Lanpher at that time. The program aired on Minnesota Public Radio. I invited Meg Bale, former social worker for Children's Home Society of Minnesota, to do the live interview with me. It was a spirited discussion. We talked about the emotional aspects of giving up one's baby for adoption, believing to never be connected with the child again. I spoke of the "unwed mother" experience. We explored aspects of identity, grief, and loss and discussed the changes open adoption has brought. Meg said something during that interview that I will never forget. "Children can handle anything," she said, "as long as it is the truth." What a wonderful lesson.

Not long after that radio interview, I received a phone call from the History Theatre in St. Paul. Ron Peluso, the artistic director, had heard me on MPR and said, "We have to talk." He invited me to meet with him. My first thought was, "This never happens." And it doesn't. But it did. That meeting with Ron was the start of two years of intense research, culminating in the performance of the play, *Watermelon Hill*, which was inspired by *Shadow Mothers* and, "Watermelon Hill," my poem about being unmarried, pregnant and living at a "home for unwed mothers."

Throughout the process, Ron was always generous, professional and deeply kind to me. It was good of him to include me in virtually all aspects of creating the play. I knew nothing about theater and was amazed to learn how a play is developed, start to finish. The first thing Ron did was to hire Lily Baber Coyle as playwright, after making sure I agreed with the choice. At our first meeting, Lily had already done some research and written a draft of a treatment, which was pretty impressive. After Lily was on board, she and I spent hours together, finding pertinent people, interviewing them and clarifying facts. At Ron's direction, Lily wrote draft after draft of the play. Ron kept saying, "Go back to the book, Lily. Go back to the book." He knew what he was looking for and knew how to get it.

Lily and I met with Dr. Crutchfield, the doctor who delivered my son in 1966. He had been in his residency then, and "the home" was part of his rotation. Dr. Crutchfield was exactly as I remembered him—gentle and caring. I was surprised to hear that he remembered me from all those years ago. Ironically, the day Lily and I met with the doctor was my birth son's birthday. That meeting was another reunion, of sorts. I wasn't surprised to learn that he tried to get Mother Superior to feed us healthier food. "All that meatloaf and canned food . . . all that sodium." he said. Mother Superior's response was, "These girls aren't here for a picnic, you know. These girls have done wrong." That statement says a lot about the attitude of the times. The more shocking news that Dr. Crutchfield shared with us was that, after delivery, the doctors were instructed to "sew the girls up nice and tight," so their future husbands wouldn't know they'd had a baby. We weren't supposed to tell anyone, ever. Small wonder so many of us are damaged beyond belief.

With Lily and I taking careful notes, we found and met with other people connected with "the home," including birthmothers, nuns, a priest, and social workers. The famous (or should I say, infamous) Sister Jane McDonald, had worked there, and took on our cause with a passion. During our informational meetings, she would often lead us in song and usually shed some tears over the injustice that had been done to "the girls."

WATERMELON HILL

Close the door and never look back.
This is finished for you now.
—Sister Marie Dolores

After she got herself in trouble, they sent her
away to Watermelon Hill, which was not really
its name, but what the boys yelled to the swollen girls
who were to come due at that home for unwed mothers.
A crucifix glared from the roof.
Laurel Taylor was not her real name.
What was real was absolved by Mother
Superior with a flap of her cloak.
Under the Immaculate Heart of Mary
was posted a litany of daily chores.
Miles of buffed linoleum, bars on the windows,
Doctor Crutchfield on Wednesdays, jelly jars
filled with vitamins. The tables were set for forty
or so, depending on who was in labor.
The tuna casseroles smelled like bleach.
Girls back from the hospital sat on donut pillows.
Days passed and the moon sickened.
Laurel Taylor, on her horrible cot with the stars
moving inside her, tried to pray.
It was best to give up your baby, not see or hold it.
It was best to place your baby, make a plan for it.

Laurel Taylor tried to pray in the chapel,
her cardigan sweater open like a gate.
She fought to be good, to give her blood to some
nice family, to cleanse a child from her name.
Laurel Taylor tried to keep the monsters away
but under some god's baleful eye, they rose
in a spine-cramping pain that was only the start
of the tearing off.

She lost her son in that war. Wading in water,
being able to see her feet again, she knew there would be
no anointing, no Extreme Unction.
After signing the surrender, she knew
the penance is fault and the loss is eternal.

January 27, 2001, was opening night for the play, *Watermelon Hill.* Although I had attended most of the auditions and rehearsals, I wasn't prepared for my own emotions while I witnessed parts of my life unfold on the stage. It was uncomfortable, thrilling and profound all at the same time. While signing autographs after each performance, I met women and men who were so moved by the play they had tears in their eyes.

I felt humbled. Five years earlier, when I was writing into the darkness and pain of my own story, along with the stories of the other women, I had no idea how other people would react. I had no idea how important that work was going to be. So you see, I am very lucky.

To Shine the Light

by Kate St. Vincent Vogl, author of *Lost & Found: A Memoir of Mothers*

I FIRST MET LINDA BACK MCKAY at a dinner for teachers at the Loft Literary Center, a nationally renowned writing community. It was my first time teaching at the Loft, so I knew no one at the event. Fortunately, there was an empty seat at the far end of Linda's table. A fellow instructor asked what I was working on, and I told her about writing a memoir about my birthmother finding me through my mom's obituary.

"You have to meet Linda," she said. She was right.

During the writing of my memoir I felt alone in my story and isolated in my adoption experience. Yet here at this very table was a kind woman who showed me pictures of the son she had surrendered at birth and the daughter she had adopted, along with her other beloved children. I was struck by her warmth and generosity—her willingness to be open to the universe and all the good it offers.

When I read her story in *Shadow Mothers*, I was overcome by the same reactions. The fact that she has maintained her strength of spirit despite the horrible circumstances of her younger years is amazing to me.

This collection of stories touches anyone whose life has been touched by adoption in any way. Though readers may come to these pages certain they are alone in their experiences, the women within these stories have known the same love, loneliness, ostracism, despair and, despite it all, hope. The hope that the one you've lost on the other side of the adoption triad knows the love you carry.

Linda has given me so much, I will need many lives just to begin to repay her. She connected me with the wonderful publisher, North Star Press. Joy of all joys, they wanted my book. Linda took me under her wing as my memoir went to press and was always supportive and wise in her counsel to me. We have shared readings, presentations and classes together, and I remain humbled by her generosity and wisdom.

Nowhere has this been more apparent than in the play, *Watermelon Hill*, inspired by Linda's story and staged at the History Theatre in St. Paul, Minnesota. Even after a successful run, the playwright remained so taken by the stories within *Shadow Mothers,* that she went on to write a musical version. I was lucky enough to be in the audience for a reading and I loved every minute of it. Lily Baber Coyle truly brought the words to life. To have your story recreated on stage is a dream for any writer. I will confess I was glad I had come alone, because I dissolved into tears many times that night—and I wasn't alone. Everyone in my row was dabbing their eyes when the lights came up.

About a year later, Linda and I appeared together on a radio program called "Good Enough Moms." As Linda shared her poem, "Watermelon Hill," the rest of us in the studio silently wept, trying not to snuffle into our mics, so moved we were by her words and the history behind them.

And so it is with Linda's writing. She brings insight and tenderness to the stories she tells. This is an achievement for which all writers strive. Since Linda and I first connected—or maybe because Linda and I connected, I've been fortunate enough to share my story across the country. But I still look to her to shine the light on the path I follow. I am honored to share in the renewal of this important work.

All Our Relations

by Margaret Hasse, author of *Milk and Tides*

IN 2011 LINDA BACK MCKAY, Kate St. Vincent Vogl and I came together to teach a workshop at The Loft Literary Center. The workshop's goal was to encourage women to write about their roles in what we call the adoption triangle. We shared time with a group of interesting, diverse women, writing together and hearing stories each person had on her mind and in her heart about adoption—as birthmothers, adoptees, adoptive mothers or as more than one of these.

The work we did that day brought to light the difficulties, sadness, joys, fears and complexities of adoption. I believe that Linda's original *Shadow Mothers* book accomplished a great deal in bringing the mysteries of adoption to light. This brave book and the play inspired by it has been a gift for many women, offering understanding and relief from guilt, shame, anger, and most of all, from silence.

When Linda offered me, for this updated and new book, a chance to contribute an essay from the perspective of an adoptive mother, I thought first of the deep and inextricable connection between two mothers who metaphorically stand together looking with love and keen concern into the basinet of a child. If one of these mothers, the birthmother, is seen as a shadow, then the other, the adoptive mother, might be an over-exposed image whose behavior is susceptible to being publicly witnessed and judged.

Society holds some negative opinions about adoptive parents because we participate in a transaction of inequality. Some people believe we're damaged goods since infertility or the loss of a biological child may have contributed to our desire to adopt, making the adopted child second best for us. Others simply cannot believe that our bond as mothers to a child of adoption could be as complete as to a child of our bodies. On the other hand, we can be wrongly glorified as selfless people who take on "needy" children. Adoptive mothers sometimes share a sense of being misunderstood, too. In response to negative or unrealistic views cast over the adoptive mother, I offer not arguments or a consistent narrative, but a few fragments and ideas from my own experience:

Over the past two decades, I've been the day-by-day mother of two boys that I did not gestate or birth. These are my sons. They are mine, delivered to me through the decision of the birthmothers, the labor and privilege of taking care of them, being with them, loving them in person for a span of time that now exceeds 7,000 days.

Of course, my boys are also the sons of women who were distressed and optimistic enough to make, as the expression goes, an adoption plan for their babies. I never forget Chawni and Lisa. I feel forever linked to them. They are part of a web of my children's relations and of mine. I was chosen by them to be a mother. My gratitude to them is truly beyond what I am able to express, yet I continue giving voice through poetry to what I feel about them.

BASKET, RIVER

A baby placed
in a well-woven basket
of adoption
moves with the flow
that carries its little life
from one woman
to another whose arms
are ready to tend,
whose body has remained empty
of what she is in need of carrying,
who plucks the bundle
from among the bulrushes,
out of the stream.

I stand at the river,
thinking of the woman
upstream, how in the middle
of hardship and loss,
she had faith
in a small basket, a big river,
that someone with strong arms
would pull her beloved son
from the current, lift him high,
raise him to manhood,
the child of two mothers
who labored in different ways
believing in water's unbroken stream.

An adoptive mother can be threatened by the thought of the first mother, fearing that the biological imperative of nature will trump the bond with a child created through nurture. Throughout my life as a mother, gratitude, and a deep current of connection with the birthmothers have been my prevailing feelings, but I, too, have had some conflicting emotions. Fear and protectiveness were strongest during the time before the adoption was finalized. I had a child in my arms I was totally in love with, but whom I might be called upon to relinquish. Could I find courage, as a birthmother had, to place a baby into another woman's arms? I hoped so, yet the following poem shows how immediately I attached to the baby I'd been given and how much I wanted to keep him.

MARKING HIM

Does my little son miss the smell
of his first mother? I wonder
as the mewl of his mouth
opens toward a plastic bottle
that is not her breast.

Sudden new mother
I bury my nose deep
into his skullcap of ringlets,
his starry cheesiness.

In her good-bye letter to him
sealed in his album
with a birth certificate, which now
lists my name as Mother,

his first mother writes
she nursed him briefly
after he emerged into
the second room of his world.

I think of milk, volcanic
and insistent, answering
the newborn's gigantic thirst,
a primal agreement between
generosity and greed.

Sometimes I press my nose
to the glass of that place
where a mother and my child
belong to each other;
I cannot imagine coming
between them.

But then I want to lick him all over
with a cow's thick tongue,
to taste him and mark him as mine
so if the other mother returns,
she will refuse her handled calf
smeared with my smell.

"Marking Him" provoked an angry reaction from a reader. The woman, who identified herself in an email as a biological mother of four, said it was selfish and offensive of me to write about separating a legitimate mother and her child. Since illegitimate is the opposite of the adjective she used, I wondered it she were against adoption in any circumstance? Or perhaps the raw intensity of my desire to belong with this child, conveyed in such a visceral way, put her off through its needy or greedy tone?

I cannot imagine loving any child from my body any more than I love my sons. But all adoptions are permeated with losses, even as they lead to new experiences and discoveries for everyone involved.

Some adoptive parents decide to pursue adoption after learning they are infertile or after a child's death. A child who died is part of the spiritual circle of my family. I didn't choose to adopt children to replace a lost biological child. Everyone and every situation are unique and valuable in their own right. Loss and love can both soften and enlighten us. Grieving for what we lost does not diminish us, but can actually increase our appreciation and commitment to what we have.

In one of his earliest stick drawings of our family of four, my younger son drew in a fifth little person with a pink heart. He called her the ghost girl. She resembled a guardian angel or a moth drawn to the light of the living. His drawing prompted me to write this poem about subjects that used to be considered taboo—miscarriage, the search for the right balance between thinking of what might have been while being alive to the present, and something adoptive parents are bound to think about at some point, which is the loss of our particular genetic message.

Her Place in Our Summer World

> In my dream, the ultrasound shows
> the dark clot that is not a child
> who would be six this summer.
> Done with kindergarten,

her class picture might show
freckles, like mine, on the bridge
of her nose—faint stars that vanish
in the morning. No,

she was just a fistful of cells that stopped
going anywhere after the first trimester.
The doctor pointed to her image,
blighted nebula, the limits of her
disintegrating into a black hole.

Then the doctor scraped
and she was gone. But
would she have loved horses as I did,
dressing miniature palominos in saddles;
undressing them, letting them loose
on the carpet to caper and graze?

I cannot think of her for too long
in light of my living sons
who came through the determination
of adoption because we did not get her.

On opposite ends of a teeter-totter,
two kinds of children lift and descend.
On one seat, my never-never daughter.
On the other, two lively sons sit
on this side of life solid as stones,
catapulting her to the edge of thought.

From the very start, when the boys were babies, I talked with them about their birthmothers. I wanted to convey how brave these women were. I explained that each of their birthmothers was a single woman who decided that a couple could provide better care for them. I wanted them to feel a live link with women whose life and decisions brought them into being and impacted their lives, perhaps for the best.

I showed the boys pictures of their birthmothers and, when they were old enough, asked if they wanted to put them in frames on their desks. One liked this idea, the other didn't care for it—but he didn't want a picture of me on his desk either.

"I'm not a picture person," he said.

Over the years, I wrote many letters to my son's birthmothers, letting them know about the developments of our shared sons. I sent pictures, then drawings by the children. At first I worried that correspondence might cause too much pain, reminding them of what they were missing. Although our adoptions were legally "closed," each birthmother had asked me not only to send news of her son, but also to remain open to a face-to-face relationship. I remain open to this.

Over the years, Chawni, my oldest son's birthmother, wrote to assure me that she wanted letters and information. She sent birthday cards. At her request, we met when our son was about eight years old and expressed interest in seeing his birthmother. The playground meeting went well, but neither mother nor child asked to meet again. They are not in contact now, almost fifteen years later, although there's always potential for re-connection.

Birthday cards continued for a few more years. Then—surprise—a birth announcement arrived: her second child, a girl, my son's half-sister. (Isn't there a better term than doesn't suggest truncation?) Although still without a supportive mate, Chawni felt more able to raise this child. When our son did not receive a birthday card that year, he shrugged it off.

"That's the way it is," he said. "New babies get all the attention."

Lisa, our other son's birthmother, had also asked for regular letters, but was more cautious, stipulating that the letters be sent to our shared adoption agency, which would in turn, forward them to her. After a few years, she moved and didn't provide the agency with her new address. My updates, which I continued to write and send, wait in the agency's files in case she makes contact again. Ironically, it's her birth child who longs for contact with her. He is now old enough to begin a search for her, with our full support.

Although each boy had his own way of coming to terms with his identity and the place of a birthmother in his life, they both grew into young men comfortable claiming adoption as part of their uniqueness. When they were very little, it would have been too much to expect them to understand the concept of two mothers. Back then, they created their own origin stories, including one that shows a child claiming the mother he knew best—me—as his own.

Might this expression of an adopted child's exclusionary love for the new mother be painful for a birthmother to hear? At the same time, might it bring her relief? Would she agree that close bonding with the adoptive mother is essential for the child's security and well-being? I hope she would find comfort in it.

After I Tell My Four-Year-Old Son the Story of His Adoption, He Counters With His Own Version

> *When I was a baby fifty years ago,*
> *when the dinosaurs all died of a heart attack,*
> *there was no birthmother.*
> *That's when I lived inside you, Mommy,*
> *and came out of you—*
> *the prettiest girl in the whole wild world.*
> *And then I went to the hospital to get fixed.*
> *Then I came home as a little guy on fast legs*
> *and started running and having fun ha ha.*

To Cherish the Moments

by Ethna McKiernan, author of *Sky Thick with Fireflies*

When *Shadow Mothers* was originally published in 1998, I was deeply moved by the book on several levels—the importance of its content, the bravery it took for those contributors to come forward with their stories, and the fact that, at last, truth was being spoken in a culture of silence, which has kept birthmothers from speaking out and sometimes even acknowledging their very loss. I was grateful, too, that many reunions had occurred between adult children and their original mothers—a joyful miracle.

Perhaps more than anything, I was personally moved because that year my youngest child was six years old, having lived with his adoptive parents since he was two days old. I was still too raw to even consider a contribution to this book, despite my unexpected good fortune of falling into an unplanned open adoption when my son was a year old. The book comforted me and validated my own experiences.

Though it's no longer the 1950s or 1960s when girls were whisked away to their "aunt's" house in another state and no one spoke of the event or loss again, there is still a terrible stigma about placing a child for adoption. More than anything, there is a sense of loss, followed by failure, followed by shame. It's still not a topic anyone readily converses about. No one sends cards or brings a casserole or flowers when we come home from the hospital empty-handed. We imagine the banners on the house of the new parents who've received our children, and their joy. We cry in private and go on because we have to. And when we don't culturally acknowledge such a loss, we can't grieve properly. All the loss burrows inward like a hundred painful missiles at once. And the missiles are hard to remove.

BIRTHMOTHER TO HER SLEEVE

I've lost you since the day that you began.
Small spark begun as love, you changed
to inconvenience as you grew, your kinsman
father running toward the exit as arranged.

Small spark begun as love, you changed
from infant into boy. Great joy
you brought another family as arranged,
black grief I knew like Troy.

From infant into boy you caused great joy
for someone else. Not me. I missed you always
in the black grief I knew like Troy;
ruined, I unlearned the verb *to pray*.

For someone else, not me, you bloomed always,
no inconvenience as you grew, your kinsman
father ignorant of the verb *to pray*.
I've lost you since the day that you began.

I spent the first year of my youngest child's life utterly wiped out by grief. I remember little of that summer except the feeling of swimming underwater and watching everyone above in a kind of disassociated state. I was hospitalized for depression but with the responsibility of two other young children at home (I was a single mother) and a small business to run, I entered the rote state of just putting one foot in front of the next. I dreamed about my baby almost daily, and the idea of nineteen years before I might see him was a painful eternity.

During that time I had much family help. My in-town sisters and friends stepped up to contribute whatever they could from cleaning to babysitting. My California brother sent us all air tickets for a ten-day visit for the boys and myself. My seventy-seven-year-old father deepened his incredible involvement with each of his grandchildren to give particular attention to mine. Under my father's supervision, my ex-husband began taking the boys more frequently as my inability to rise above a slump-pile of grief became more apparent. It was a difficult time for my two other boys, who were too young to understand the loss of adoption, but old enough to know something was really wrong with Mom. Before the baby's birth, I had taken the boys to a child psychologist to process the upcoming loss. They were young enough only to write "goodbye and good luck" letters to the baby. "I hope you have a good crib and a pet," wrote my oldest child.

I'm not sure how to bring my son's birthfather into all of this. We were in love, but it was all wrong. He suggested adoption when I was eight months pregnant, and again, I sleepwalked through that time. I had run out of strength and he was unwilling to provide any. It was complicated. My sister called him when our baby was born, but he never responded. Nor has he made any effort to contact our son. He went on to have another son, and that's about all I know.

Shortly before my baby's first birthday, I wrote his adoptive parents a letter in care of the adoption agency, asking if we could meet just one time so I could see him, meet them, and have them meet me. Amazingly and generously, they agreed to a picnic at a nearby park. It was an emotional evening for us all, and the questions flew back and forth. It turned out they had both grown up in large Irish-Catholic families, as I had. And, they lived less than three miles away. By the end of the evening we agreed to see each other again, with no ground-rules set and no road map for an accidental open adoption.

Brian's parent were clearly in love with him. That first Christmas they invited me over and gave me a video of him, and I gave them the kindergarten and first grade photos of my other sons. I sometimes reeled with gratitude to find myself a small part of my baby's life, and sometimes cried because I couldn't have a greater part.

Uncertainty reared its head along the way for both parties. There were periods when my several-times-yearly presence was threatening, and other periods when I couldn't bear walking out their door without my son.

Somehow we managed, all of us in agreement that this was the wisest and healthiest thing to give our son. At three years old, Brian knew I was his "birthmother," and called me Ethna.

Because I so hate the generic term "birthmother," I need to digress a moment. Being referred to as this made me feel an inanimate stand-in, less than a "real" mother, just as the term "adoptive mother" is also reductive, a verbal sign that she is somehow less than the child's "real" mother. It devalues us both. I don't have replacement words just yet, just my passionate belief that we are both this child's mothers, and always will be. I wish more than anything for more dialogue between both sets of parents.

THREE WISHES FOR BRIAN

That
you know your belovedness
to each mother

Whom you own;
to the father who claimed you
as a falling star

Prized
among multitudes
of hot silver;

To your brothers
who have high-fived
the toddler-photo of you

Holding a fish
for years now as they've passed it
on the refrigerator door.

##

Child
of my heart, how you've grown
into your long-stemmed body!

Four-and-a-half-years
tall, five years later, your
glad spirit

Bells, bends
each of our lives with music
I can at last and only

Call joy.

Though I've had the chance to be in my child's life to some degrees, I feel we have a long way to go in actually knowing each other. Now that he's nineteen, I don't see his adoptive parents as much, and when he shows up alone for a celebration of his birthday I have sometimes felt he's there because he's dutiful and polite. That said, nineteen is pretty young to expect depth in a complicated relationship, and I know we both need time to grow into this. I try not to compare myself to a friend who also lost her son to adoption and then later formed an incredible adult relationship with him, with the boy even naming *his* first child after my friend's beloved father.

In Brian's childhood, there were moments I treasure with him and his two brothers, including a sleepover or two in our house in which he and Conor played chess and we all watched *Searching for Bobby Fisher*. That night I put Brian to sleep in a sleeping bag next to Conor's bed, and woke at 4:00 A.M. to find him wrapped in a blanket outside my bedroom door. We had a number of other get-togethers—some highly memorable ones. Bumper cars. Movies. Valley Fair. I have a photograph I treasure of the three boys together at Brian's parents' house, rolling and tumbling and laughing in a big knot on the floor. Recently Brian and my two older children had an animated discussion of music during a visit, and I wanted to freeze-frame the moment, the three of them talking and laughing. And during a dinner out with Brian and his lovely girlfriend, I also wanted to freeze-frame the moment he told me they were engaged. I cherish these small moments of closeness, and want again to express my enormous gratitude to his parents, who took an unconventional and risky leap into the unknown by welcoming me back into his life.

For all of you who had the courage to contribute to this book, and to Linda Back McKay for originating it, I offer thanks.

Introduction

by Marti Erickson, Ph.D., Director Emerita, Harris Training Programs, University of Minnesota

FOR SEVERAL YEARS MY DAUGHTER Erin and I have co-hosted a talk show originally called *Good Enough Moms,* now *Mom Enough*™ (*www.momenough.com*). We address the many facets of motherhood— the ups and downs of childrearing, the struggle to find a healthy balance between mothering and other aspects of our lives, how society views and values mothers and mothering. We describe our mission as "supporting you to be the mom your children need, the woman you want to be" (easy to say, hard to do!). Although we each bring some professional credentials to our show (me as a developmental psychologist and university researcher who has studied parent-child relationships for decades, my daughter as a maternal-child health specialist in the field of public health), we also feature guests who are experts in a variety of topics related to child development, health, mental health and family relations. And we always are on the lookout for mothers with a story to tell that will shed light on some particular aspect of motherhood and mothering.

A couple of years ago we heard about two extraordinary books that offered striking and complementary views of a motherhood story we had not addressed, that of birthmothers who had given their babies up for adoption. Yes, we had done shows about adoption, including processes of adopting, the challenges adopted children often face, and the importance of supportive resources for adoptive families. But we had not discussed the mothers who bore these adopted children. As we have come to learn since, we were not alone in overlooking that crucial aspect of the broader stories about adoption. So, we invited the authors of the two books to join us in the studio for what turned out to be one of the most deeply moving shows we ever have done. The authors were Linda Back McKay and Kate St. Vincent Vogl, who used their own stories and those of others to bring out of the shadows the varied and complex experiences of birth mothers (and in Vogl's case, the adopted daughter whose birth mother found her, regardless of whether she wanted to be found).

The remarkable stories of these two authors—and of the various birth mothers who provided their stories for Linda Back McKay's *Shadow Mothers*—call into question what it really means to be a mother and illuminate how many different answers there are to that question, depending on time, culture, and circumstances. These stories also raise profound questions about how our society views women, including our ambivalence about women's sexuality (i.e. how we objectify and sexualize females from an early age even as we shame and chastise them for acting on that sexuality). These stories also raise questions about the right to know and to be known, both as it applies to birth parents and the children they yield to another family.

Granted, the birthmothers who tell their stories in the original *Shadow Mothers* and in this welcome new edition, *Out of the Shadows*, are speaking of a time when attitudes toward unwed mothers were much harsher and the options for those women were far fewer. But one doesn't have to dig too deeply to find the same kind of scrutiny, shame, and judgment in our society today. And, of course, as the stories themselves reveal, the legacy of these women's experiences are here and now, continuing today to affect the women, their children, and those around them.

I am of the same generation as most of the birthmothers who tell their stories here. Although I hate to admit it, I was one of the high school girls in the early 1960s who listened eagerly to whispered rumors about the classmate who had gone to live with her aunt in another town for the rest of the school year. I remember driving by a home for unwed mothers near the town where I lived, looking at the bleak building with the bars on the windows and feeling both pity for—and curiosity about—the girls inside. How did they end up there and why? What would become of them and their babies? But, frankly, I really never paused to imagine the experience of carrying a baby for nine months, enduring the pains of labor and childbirth only to let go of that baby and relinquish all claim to his or her future. I never imagined the loss—not only in that moment, but on each subsequent birthday and at each milestone or developmental passage (first steps, first words, the start of school, graduation, marriage). Back then I never stopped to imagine the shame, the secrecy, and the loneliness those girls experienced, nor certainly the enduring impact on the young women and their subsequent children and partners.

In my adult life, however, as a developmental psychologist and researcher studying intergenerational cycles of parenting, I have witnessed countless times how emotions denied will fester and hurts unspoken will destroy. I see now that was the fate of so many of those young women who were set aside, sewn up tight, told to swallow their feelings and keep their secrets. Their stories need to be told, for the women's sake and that of their children and other loved ones, and I thank Linda Back McKay for making that happen. You and I also need to hear their stories and see through these women's eyes, regardless of whether adoption is part of our own life story. Understanding these mothers—their heartaches and their joys—is the first step in making sure no young woman has to live her life in the shadows again.

Chapter One

I WAS SICK A LOT WHEN I WAS A KID, and completely wrapped up in my own little world, as children sometimes are. I was boisterous and outgoing. "Don't be so loud!" was probably the phrase I heard most often.

People said I looked just like Elizabeth Taylor and I believed them. I loved pretending that I was a star, and once staged a circus in a vacant lot for charity with my friends and my wonder-dog, Chips. People actually came! We made a lot of money and sent it to the Damon Runyon Foundation, an organization for helping sick children. The Foundation even sent us a thank you note, too.

Our extended family and everyone we knew lived nearby. Our neighborhood in the late 1940s and early 1950s was like a small town, although it was part of New York City. Surrounded by caring aunts, uncles, cousins, family friends, and my big sister Alicia Jo, who looked like Grace Kelly, I was confident of my place in the world.

Except for when my dad was out of town on one of his many business trips. Then I was desolate. I'd get stomachaches so bad that Mom would have to take me to Dr. Cohen, who thought that my mom should try to find someone who could act as a surrogate dad for me. Mom asked Mr. Melvin, who tried his best, letting me sit in his lap and making a fuss over me. I don't think he was very comfortable in the role, though, and neither was I. I think Mr. Melvin's daughter resented it, too, so we gave it up. The stomachaches eventually went away, but not until I was an adult.

I remember when Dad used to let my sister and me comb his hair into ridiculous styles while he'd make a funny face to heighten the effect. And I remember us climbing onto Mom and Dad's big bed on Saturday mornings to wake him up for breakfast, with the sweet smell of bacon wafting from the kitchen.

Mom was a nurse and worked full time, but in my memory she was always there. She took Alicia Jo and me to the pool on hot summer days, and when we couldn't use the public pool because of the polio epidemic, she set up the lawn sprinkler in the yard for us. I remember exactly how she smelled in her satin gown when she would kiss us goodnight before she and Dad went out to the Masonic Hall. It was a heady combination of cigarettes, Tabu perfume, and Clorets.

One of my best childhood memories is when I discovered that my sister liked me. Alicia Jo was the smartest person on the planet and three years older than me. I figured she hated me because she always ditched me when I tried to play with her. But when I became very sick with encephalitis and needed to be taken to the hospital, she sat with me for hours, telling little stories and playing little games to try to keep me awake, because they didn't want me to go into a coma before Dr. Cohen got there. After that, no matter what happened between us, I always knew that she really cared about me.

My whole life changed when we moved from New York to a town just west of Minneapolis, Minnesota. I was ten and we knew only a few people—some of Mom's relatives. There weren't any Angellinis, Picarellos, or Cohens, either. Everybody was blonde as lutefisk and had absolutely no accent.

I didn't fit in—the way I looked (I was short and round with black hair), the way I talked (I had a lisp in addition to the New York accent) and the way I acted (loud and obnoxious). I had zero friends. I did have my Arthur Godfrey guitar, though, and I could sing pretty well. I think I acted the way I did to get attention, but it never really worked the way I wanted.

In junior high school, I met Kay. She was loud like me, beautiful, talented and funny. We were a striking pair—Kay was as blonde as I was dark. She thought I was beautiful and funny, too. We shared a rather strange sense of humor, joking about almost everything, including her father's accidental death in the basement of her home, and the fact that she was adopted. We spent all our free time together—usually at her house.

Kay lived with her mother and older brother, and together we listened to classical music and discussed subjects like history and politics. At home, if I tried to state an opinion about grown-up subjects like that, Dad would tell me, "You're not old enough to have an opinion." And, "When I want to hear what you think, I'll let you know."

But at Kay's house, my opinion and input was always welcomed.

I worked very hard at trying to fit in at school. I tried out for the cheerleading team and made it. Kay never seemed to worry about fitting in. We joined the Thespian Club together and got some meaty roles because of our acting talents. We were inseparable.

By the time I was a junior, I was starting to believe that I fit in just fine when I really wanted to. Unfortunately, that positive sense of self was short lived.

Will, a senior, came from New York like me. His family was wealthy, interesting and well educated, and their house was full of art. His mom was an artist and a poet. I wanted a life like theirs. Will played football, but had kind of an aloof attitude with the other kids. He was a very cool guy and listened to jazz.

As it turns out, Will was not a nice boy. He didn't tell me that he already had a girlfriend and only wanted me for sex. I thought we were going steady and desperately wanted to please him. After the first time we had sex, Will told me I was not very good at it, and that I should get some experience and come back and see him when I knew what I was doing. I guess that's why I spent the next few months having sex with just about anyone who would have me. Or maybe it was because I wanted someone to love me, even if it was just for five minutes.

Kay was having sex with a lot of guys, too, and she always made a big joke out of it. When she suggested a competition to see which of us could have sex with the most guys that summer, the race was on! I had become that dreaded word, a slut. I remember getting ready to leave for a party and Dad telling me to go back upstairs and scrub my face. "You look like a French whore," he said.

Many years later, I learned that my deep need for reassurance caused me to somehow punish myself with my own sexuality. The result was a growing sense of self-loathing.

I went to Zion Lutheran Church every Sunday with Mom and my sister, while Dad took his Sunday morning bath. He had always been very active in our old congregation, but he never set foot in a church after we left Staten Island. I wasn't sure why.

During my senior year, I met Al, who said he loved me in spite of everything I had done. Al was a Baptist who promised to save me from myself. After graduation, I started at the University of Minnesota with Kay, just as we had always planned. But nothing felt real. I'd come home on weekends and pretend everything was fine, but nothing was fine. Dad had a girlfriend and my sister and I knew it. I think my mother knew. But she was pretending that everything was fine, too.

Al worked at a gas station, didn't want a college education, and didn't think I should have one either. Especially if we were to be married. I convinced myself that marrying Al would make everything okay. I remember our Lutheran minister coming to the house the night before I was to be married, trying to talk me out of this "terrible mistake." He said I would be damning my unborn children to hell, because Baptists don't baptize infants. As it turned out, I had no children in that marriage, so no souls were at risk. Except my own.

It was a huge wedding with a beautiful white gown and hundreds of guests. We spent money my parents didn't have—and just in time for Dad to walk me down the aisle before leaving Mom for a younger woman.

Al abused me physically, worked me like a slave and ran around with other women. We were managing a moderately priced motel. I did all the laundry, supervised the cafe and handled the books. My health began to suffer, and my doctor said I should leave my husband if he wouldn't let me rest more. When I told Al I wanted to leave, he advised me that I'd be leaving God, not just the marriage, and that staying married to him was my only chance at salvation. Lonely and desperate, I had an affair with Rick, the night manager, who was college educated and sympathized with me about how bad things were with Al. He also thought I was smart.

When I finally got up the courage to leave Al, I approached Mom for a place to stay. Mom had her own problems trying to make a life for herself without Dad. Kay knew everything about what had been going on. She and her mother offered to take me in until my mom could handle my coming home, which ended up being only a few days. That was a good time, actually, for Mom and me, Chips, and my cat, Sam. I got a job at the hospital where Mom was a nurse, and we drove to work together every day. We were pretty broke and awfully sad, but we shared it all together.

Unfortunately, my judgment hadn't improved, and I kept letting men mess up the picture. I fell in love with Rick, but I was still married to Al, and Rick was still married, too, and still living with his wife. It was all very tawdry, but I put a great deal of energy into making everything work out. Kay knew about all of this, too, and kept trying to introduce me to younger, more eligible guys. She'd invite me to parties and set up double dates and I'd go, telling lies to Rick along the way.

One night at a party, Kay ran into a guy she was interested in, and I said I'd be able to get a ride home. A guy named Bill was all too glad to take me home. He just had to stop by his house on the way to pick up something. And would I just run in with him for a minute? He did take me home—several hours later.

That morning in my own bed, I knew what happened but I didn't remember it. I couldn't remember drinking enough to explain the loss of memory, either. I discovered I was pregnant about a month later. I wasn't positive if Bill was the father or if it was Rick, but it was probably Rick.

I went into hiding. We didn't let anyone know—not my dad, not even my sister at first. Just Mom, Rick, Kay, and I were in on it. From the very beginning, I knew this baby would be adopted by someone who could give him a good future. The best thing I could do was to hide my pregnancy, and make sure the family in New York never knew, to spare my mother the shame. I thought I would pick up my life again after the baby was born—that my life would continue as if it never happened. After all, that's exactly what Kay had done the year before, and she seemed to be fine, still laughing and joking as usual. Kay would be there to help me through it all.

Rick and I rented an apartment on the outskirts of Minneapolis where we didn't know anybody. My cat and I lived there, and Rick stayed there sometimes. Mom brought me groceries and spent time with me when she could, but I could see how disappointed she was in me.

The other people in the apartment building thought my husband worked out of town. They were very kind to me, and even surprised me with a baby shower—which, of course, was the last thing I wanted.

When Rick could get away from his wife he'd come for me, and I'd lie on the floor of the car so I wouldn't be seen on the way to the drive-in movie. Those movies were the only times I'd leave the apartment. Kay stopped by often to play cribbage, make popcorn and watch TV with me. Our friendship was the most important part of my life.

I was eight months pregnant when Kay was killed. She had just turned twenty-one and was the victim of a head-on collision with a drunk driver. I was told that she probably died quickly and didn't suffer. I couldn't go to her funeral because I was still in hiding. I remember long nights at my window, watching the distant lights of the airport on the otherwise black horizon.

When my labor pains started, Rick drove me to the big new hospital on the south side of town. Mom met us there and all the good things I remember about that day have to do with Mom. She was my guardian, defender, private-duty nurse, and advocate. Mine was going to be one of the first babies born at that hospital and the staff was planning to make a big to-do about it—until they realized my circumstances.

When it was time to take me to the delivery room, the nurse who was taking care of me said sarcastically, "Great! This is just what I needed right now!"

After my son was born, I asked to count his fingers and toes and make sure his body was normal. I had heard that people did not adopt babies who were not perfect. If there had been something wrong with him I would have kept him, rather than let him spend his life in an institution. He was perfect. I let them take him away, knowing I would never see him again. I didn't let myself feel much emotion. I wanted everything to be over. Years later, I thought I must have been the coldest person in the world, but it was all I could do then. Maybe I was protecting myself.

I was placed in a double room with a married woman who had her baby and her happy family with her often. The contrast between her happiness and my emptiness was too difficult for me, and Mom managed to come up with the extra money for a private room.

A social worker came to see me, tried to convince me to hold my baby one more time and reconsider my decision to place him for adoption. Now that I look back on it, I'm sure she simply wanted to be sure I had made a well-considered decision, but at the time I thought she was being judgmental. Besides, I never did really make a decision. Giving him up was all I could do. It was what Rick wanted and what Mom needed me to do. I didn't hold my son again.

I went back to the apartment and told the people there that my baby had died. It was awful to have to keep lying, but it seemed so important at the time to protect the secret. I returned all the lovely baby gifts they had given me, endured their condolences and recuperated for a few weeks. I hated myself by then—not so much for giving up my baby, but for all the lies. I never really allowed myself to feel the loss of my baby until years later.

When the legal papers were ready, I signed them. Rick agreed to be named as father so the baby could be adopted without my husband ever knowing. Then it was all over. My baby was really gone.

After our divorces were final, Rick and I got married. We built a home and I got pregnant. Weeks passed, and the very day we signed the loan closing papers for our house, I lost the baby. The doctors said I would probably never carry a baby full term. We kept trying, but every pregnancy ended in miscarriage. I had known there'd be a price to pay and this was my punishment. I would never be allowed another child.

Our big beautiful house was full of empty rooms. We looked into adoption and even went through the initial interviews. I figured it would be an even exchange—that I deserved someone else's child since someone else had mine. But we found out that there was a two-year waiting period, and just never pursued it further.

Circumstances eventually brought children into our household. I happily welcomed Derek and Robbie, who were four and seven, into our household. Their dad, Rick's brother, had divorced his wife and moved to Saigon to run a bar for GIs—and the kids needed a home. He wouldn't let his ex-wife have them and didn't want them with him in Vietnam. But I sure wanted them.

Rick and I tried to build a life for these children and ourselves. We got involved in our community with Little League and children's choir. Rick ran for city council, and I joined a community education group that evolved into a civil rights organization. I had quit my clerking job at the insurance company to spend more time with the boys, but when Rick's business failed, it was clear I needed to work again. Through our political contacts, I found a job as bookkeeper for the state of Minnesota with a drunk driving prevention program.

Eventually my second marriage began to fall apart, slowly but surely, because it had been based on too much sorrow and guilt, and not enough friendship or love. Rick agreed to let the boys stay with me after we separated, but then their father found out. He took them away from me Fourth of July weekend 1973, with barely enough time for us to say goodbye.

The night before they left for Saigon, Robbie came into my room, sat next to me on my bed and cried inconsolably. He said, "I know that if I go away, you will die, and I'll never see you again."

Our house was so empty after Derek and Robbie left. On the day before Thanksgiving, I got the news that while the boys had been playing on a roof, Robbie fell into some high-tension wires, was electrocuted and died. He was thirteen. Like so many boys who were victims of that war, he is buried somewhere in Saigon.

I blanked out a lot of what happened after that. My dad died, and my mom moved to the West Coast. I was planning to join her, needing someone to take care of me so badly. Then I met Ben, a divorced lawyer with five teenage daughters. Mom was so proud that I was dating an attorney.

Ben reassured my mom that he knew how hard my life had been, and told her, "Trust me. She'll never have to worry about anything again."

I didn't know Ben very well when I married him, but I knew his daughters liked me. Ben thought I would be happier if we had a child together. A few months after we were married, I went to the doctor to see if it was safe to get pregnant. He informed me that I already was!

When Abby was born, I believed I had finally been forgiven. She was so wonderful! Then, a few months after her birth, I began to notice strange quirks in Ben's personality. I think he had married me to replace the "wife unit" in his life. He became verbally abusive, and had ongoing scary outbursts that were directed at either one of his daughters or me. The daughters and I helped take care of whoever's turn it was to be "it" but after they all moved out, I was "it" all the time.

I stayed for seven years, thinking it was what I deserved. After all, I had been allowed to have Abby—how greedy could I be? What right did I have to want anything more? But as time went on, I started to see what was happening at home contrast more and more with the rest of my life.

Molly, a wonderful woman who was my boss at the state of Minnesota, encouraged me to try new things. I edited the newsletter and even applied for her job when she left. I became financial officer of the project and, with the support of some friends, identified my skills as a counselor. People I talked to believed I had a knack for helping people identify their problems, and bring out their own resources to deal with them. I became a volunteer at the local rape center. Within a year I was offered a full-time job.

As a victim advocate/crisis intervention worker and community educator, I was confident in my abilities. I loved what I was doing. I was amazed by all these incredible women who were finding strength to change their lives—sometimes with my help! Yet, ironically, there I was, still stuck in yet another abusive relationship.

As I became more and more worthy in my own eyes, it became clear that I needed to leave my marriage. I left Ben for my own happiness, and so that Abby could look forward to a better life than she saw her mother having.

By that time I was thirty-five years old and fifty pounds overweight. But it was the first time since I was a little girl that I was comfortable with myself again. I was able to be a nurturing mother to Abby, who thrived physically and emotionally.

In celebration of my new independence, I hung brightly colored pieces of paper on the mirrors and walls of our new apartment that read "NO LIES!" I worked hard at my job and made wonderful friendships with women and men. Being alone and without a primary relationship with a man was better than the other ways I had lived.

Since I was finally comfortable being alone, isn't it only natural that I would finally meet the right man for me? I had first been introduced to Abe years before when he had come to visit Marta, my boss from the Rape Center. They had been friends since college and met occasionally for lunch. Abe was a nice Jewish guy—nice looking, too. But I'm sure he never noticed me. I was just another woman at the office, fifty pounds overweight and married.

Later, when I ran into Abe at a work-related party, I had lost weight and gained confidence. I asked him to dance and he refused, which was deflating, but Marta, my boss, encouraged me to pursue him. She had talked to him about me, and she said he sounded interested.

"I think you should call him and ask him to meet you for a drink," she said in her firmest boss voice.

I gave Abe a call the following week, figuring I had nothing to lose. We met at a classy old hotel bar the night of the all-star game, 1982. I didn't realize it at the time, but Abe had made a great sacrifice to meet me that night. He's a baseball fanatic. He actually weeps at the last game of the World Series because baseball is over for the season. He cries for happiness each spring at the beginning of the season, too. He did get home that night in time to catch the last few innings. As he pointed out, the all-star game doesn't really count anyway. Everybody always knows who's going to win.

Abe and I have been together since that night at the bar. I thought I'd never see him again after the night I told him I loved him. He had been married before, too. It took a very long time for either of us to trust that our relationship would work.

We live in big old house in St. Paul and work together to take care of it. Thirteen years now, and our marriage is stronger than ever. Maybe it's because we were both married before and have learned from the experience. Maybe it's because we don't need to MAKE each other happy—or MAKE each other anything. He refuses to make me respectable—he just respects me. And he loves me. Abby thinks of Abe as a third parent, and loves him very much. She celebrates Father's Day with her father and "Abe's Day" with Abe a week later.

Almost immediately after Abe, Abby, and I moved in together, it was discovered that I had a large ovarian tumor. We were terrified that I had cancer. The tumor was benign, but the scare started me thinking about my son again. Ovarian cancer is almost always fatal. What if he came looking for me and I was dead?

Ever since the laws had changed in Minnesota, allowing children to attempt to find their birthparents, I had fantasized that one day my son would find me. I thought about it every day in the shower, which was almost the only time I was alone. But I had never thought about it the other way around until the cancer scare.

I wrote to the social service agency and asked them to find my son's family and let them know that I, a stable woman (as stable as I'd ever been at least!) with a good marriage, job, and child of my own, would be open to contact with their son, if they thought it was in his best interest. His family waited for a couple months to tell him. The day after he got the news he called the agency to set up our first meeting.

It was two weeks before Christmas, the year my son turned twenty. I drove to the agency by myself, was shown to a room and seated at a table to wait. I knew his name was Justin. I've never been so nervous. I had tried to prepare myself for every possible reaction he might have to me—from hatred to anger to blame to confusion as to why I had given him up. But I wasn't prepared for what really happened.

A beautiful young man entered the room. I stood, extended my hand to him and began to cry. Ignoring my outstretched hand, he put his arms around me and held me close.

"It's all right now. It's all right," he said as he patted my back gently.

Imagine. My grown-up child comforting ME, after all I had done! Then we talked. We talked about everybody and everything.

I was overwhelmed by the familiarity of him. We had so much in common. We drove the same make of car. We even had many of the same mannerisms—like pulling at the collars of our turtlenecks. His sense of humor and mine were just the same. Justin looked just like those old pictures of Dad that mom had always kept. He looked almost exactly like my nephew. But it was more than just looks. He seemed like family. I felt like I had known him for a long, long time.

We talked about heredity and coincidence. My dad had been a jazz pianist and choir director, and my son played jazz piano and had been student director of his college choir. My dad had been an ambulance attendant in his youth and a volunteer police officer. My son had been an emergency medical technician and later became a volunteer police officer, too.

Like mine, Justin's life hasn't been easy. He's been to hell and back with his chemical dependency, and had a difficult relationship with his mother. When I showed him pictures of my father and my nephew, he said that was the first time he had seen anyone who looked like him, and that it made him feel less lonely.

He wanted me to meet his parents right away, but I was worried about doing further damage to his family life. Justin made sure that I understood that he loved his folks, and then he said, "You're in my life now and that's important to me. Our relationship has nothing to do with my folks so don't worry about it."

Kind of unrealistic, but it made me feel better.

We all gathered at a restaurant for our first meeting, which was a bit of a fiasco.

I liked Justin's girlfriend, Heidi, immediately, but his parents didn't approve of her because they were living together before marriage. There was so much tension at that table! It's hard for me to admit, but I felt resentment toward his folks. I was grateful to them for everything they had given him, but at the same time I resented them for it.

His dad, a Lutheran minister, was very kind and talked a lot about redemption that night. His mother tried to be kind, but I think she was threatened by me coming back into Justin's life. Instead of bringing photos of Justin at various ages, it seemed that all the photos were of her with him. I got the feeling that she didn't want me to forget who his real mother was. Of course I knew that she was his mother. I knew that all those years were lost to me, and that was the greatest grief of my life.

When I first told Mom about meeting Justin, she told me that she always wanted me to keep him, and never understood why I gave him up. I think we may have both rewritten history to comfort ourselves, and will never know exactly what took place back then. Mom couldn't stop crying when she first met him. She couldn't stop staring at him. He looked so much like Dad! I think it was hard on Mom when I said it was time for everybody to know about Justin, but she brags about him now.

Abby adored Justin and had known about my son ever since she was about six. I had told her the truth when she asked me, "Mom, did you ever have any other children?"

Abe and Justin are still trying to figure out their relationship, but they do have a mutual interest in music, and enjoy each other's company.

I decided that the best way for me to be part of Justin's life was to let him initiate contacts with me. That way, it's all on his terms according to his needs. But sometimes when I don't hear from him for a while, I violate my own rules and call him. We seem to need each other. When he's stressed or worried about something, he calls me to talk it over. When big things happen in his life, he wants to share them with me.

Abby, Abe, and I were at the wedding when he married Heidi. We were there with family and best friends on the terrifying night when their daughter Jessica was born prematurely at only twenty-three weeks, and again a week later when she had to have heart surgery.

Justin wanted us at the funeral when his father died, after a heart-breaking battle with brain cancer. He was very close to his adopted father, who was a strong and good man.

Justin's mother, a home economics teacher, has survived her own battle with cancer and a crippling car accident. Since her husband died, and despite all her problems, she has managed to finish her Master's degree. She is a very strong-willed woman and I've come to admire her. We have occasional phone conversations about our pride and worries regarding "our" son. Who knows—we might even end up being friends some day.

My job now is as an advocate for victims of crime in our county attorney's office. I help people deal with the effects of murder, rape, and violence of all sorts. It's exhausting but important work and I'm good at it. Weekends,

I'm often out in my perennial garden—it's good therapy for me. I also love entertaining and am a "dynamite cook," or so my friends say.

Mom lives with us now, which presents a whole new set of joys and difficulties. She turned eighty this year and is still going strong. We have much to celebrate—and host many of celebrations at our house, including an annual after-Christmas holiday with Justin, Heidi and Jessica, my miracle grandchild.

Justin, Heidi, and Jessica have moved back into his mother's house just outside of the Twin Cities. Because of her health problems, his mother was not able to maintain the home, so she had it remodeled into a duplex. They share it with her. I am proud of him for being a good son to her.

He is a wonderful son to me, too. I don't see him very often, but I know where he is, and he knows where I am. Heidi and I have a good relationship, and Jessica is a beautiful, bright, dark-eyed girl, full of life and full of herself—not unlike me as a child!

Abby has moved into her own apartment with two other young woman, and is attending technical school. She's an intelligent and lovely nineteen-year-old, still a little unsure of her place in the world. I know in my heart that she will be happy and successful in all the ways that matter.

My stepdaughters, the five girls Abby's father had when I married him, still keep in contact with us. They all have happy lives now, and bring their children to visit me every so often.

Derek, the brother of Robbie who died in Vietnam, has become a television personality, and I haven't heard from him for a while. I do sometimes speak to his uncle, Rick, who I believe is Justin's father, so I know that Derek is fine. For whatever reason, Rick does not want to meet Justin. There is nothing I can do about that, and Justin is dealing with it in his own way.

One day, Justin and Heidi invited us to join them at Heidi's parents' country home. They took us on a fun little tour of the town and I felt so happy, just being with them. In the newly remodeled town meeting hall, I found myself apart from the rest of the people, and wandered into one of the rooms. Justin was seated there at the piano, his back to me. He was playing a song I remember my dad playing in the church on Staten Island when I was a little girl. As I stood watching him, I felt as if a huge precious part of my life had been given back to me—the good memories of my father—a gift from my son.

So, life goes on. Justin's presence now is as permanent as I once thought giving him up was. For the first time, I can picture my future without dreaming of how things should be better. Being with Justin always brings a jumble of emotions. Joy because he wants me with him, pain about what has been lost, and uncertainty about what the future holds. I know I can't control anything, and I'm just trying to enjoy what is here for me now.

Chapter Two

LINDA

DANCE WITH DAD

Nothing fancy, it was like walking to him.
The Polka, the Schottische, my Mary Janes
scuffing his wing tips, his face
my Christmas tree top.

I knew all the steps. The accordion lady
played the "Blue Skirt Waltz,"
his hand and arm
the circle that turned us.

Full and humming, I knew the change would come.
On the day my father could no longer
touch me, I saw myself grown large and him
too solid for sentiment.

So the sky blows off its clouds.
After we grow up, we grow out.
After we grow out, we grow in.
It's always the loneliness that turns us.

WAS A DREAMY LITTLE KID, always pretending and fantasizing. I was "in
a world of my own," according to the aunts who gave me manicure kits
for Christmas so I'd stop biting my nails. My dolls were my real family
and the only ones who truly understood me. I had few human friends,

preferring the company of neighborhood dogs and cats. I started writing poetry as soon as I could write. My first was,

God made the birds,
God made the bees
God made my mother and God made me.
God made my father, whom I love very much.
God made my brothers, and even my old tooth brush!

I guess I've always had a big need to be understood. I wrote miniature books, illustrated them and bound them with pieces of ribbon or string. There were no other artists in our family, and I often felt like the "different" one.

My mother, like her mother and sisters, was very sentimental and caring. I remember she always felt sorry for me when I wasn't invited to a classmate's birthday party or was otherwise snubbed. My father was the strong, silent, hard-working type. Other than once a year at his labor union's Christmas dance, he spent most of his time at work in the foundry or at work in our garden. My mother canned all the vegetables he grew. Nothing went to waste.

I had two brothers. My older brother was the best and my younger brother was the cutest. We all went to St. Joseph's Catholic school. I loved

All dressed up for church in 1954.

the mystery and drama of the priests and wanted badly to be one when I grew up. But I was just a girl and girls had to be nuns, which didn't interest me much. Nuns didn't get to do the important things, like changing wine and wafers into the actual "for-real" body and blood of Christ.

Other times I felt second best were when my best friend Kathy got a real Tiny Tears doll and I got the cheaper imitation from Montgomery Wards. I desperately wanted the pearl-covered prayer book for First Communion, as well as the glimmering crystal rosary. But I had to settle for the less expensive models.

In ninth grade I was sure I was the only girl who wasn't allowed to shave her legs. I tried to wear knee-highs every day but I knew that people noticed. I dreaded gym class, when all the girls would take off their clothes. The towels they gave us were way too small and I knew my body was ugly. I tried to hold one towel in front and one in back when I went from my locker to the showers.

Everyone else seemed poised and relaxed about these things. Some even sang the song, "I'm in the nude for love . . . simply because you're near me . . . funny but—funny butt? Who's got a funny butt?"

I did pretty well in junior high and had a few friends—mostly quiet, uninspired girls. I didn't have enough confidence to do well with boys. I did have one "boyfriend" of sorts. His name was John, and whenever I talked to him his ears turned red. He walked me home from school and carried my books, but that's about it.

When I was a junior in high school I fell in love with Harry, whom I met at the Safari Club, a teenage dance hall. Harry was a member of a very exotic and harmless gang, the Ptarmigans. Gangs in those days mostly hung out together, worked on their cars and lusted after girls. Harry was a senior at another high school, and picked me up at my school in his 1964 midnight-blue Pontiac Grand Prix. I enjoyed being seen with him, driving around in that beautiful car. I remember the stirrings of all sorts of feelings inside me, and I wasn't sure exactly what they were.

Harry was my first real boyfriend and I knew we would be together forever. But after only a few months he fell in love with my friend Lindy. At our parting date he told me he was also going to get rid of his car. His car! I couldn't believe it. And then, with a knowing look, he said, "Well, everybody gets tired of everything after a while."

After that, my mother really felt sorry for me. I cried constantly, refused to go to school and spent most of my time gazing out of windows. It felt kind of good in a way, being involved in such a drama and having someone worry about me.

I wrote a poem about being made of eggshell. I felt like something was cracked or broken inside of me. I didn't care any more. Not about what I was going to do after graduation, not about anything. It was as if I didn't matter anymore. I tried to make a plan. Even enrolled in college. But my heart wasn't in it. I don't know where my heart was.

In the blur of graduation events, I went through the motions, had my senior picture taken and had some fun with classmates. That summer I worked at a candy store and arranged my transportation to college. I had to commute from St. Paul to the small Wisconsin university because we couldn't afford the dorm. I thought I'd major in English. Maybe teach some day.

I wrote poems about rolling down a hill of cotton. I didn't feel alive. As if from a distance, I liked school and was doing fairly well, but felt unfocused and vague. Slowly and deliberately, I found that sex felt good. I had a huge need to be touched and cared for. I thought that having sex meant somebody loved me. It did not take me long to find out how wrong I was.

At college, after a day of drinking beer and playing cards when we were supposed to be in class, some boys I barely knew took me out to a dark parking lot and put me in the back seat of a car. Then they raped me, one after another. I think they drugged me because I was drifting in and out of consciousness. After what seemed like hours, one of the boys took pity on me, helped me locate most of my clothes and drove me home. I'm pretty sure that was when I got pregnant. It was October 22, 1965.

The Day I Died

I wanted to be beautiful, to be known for reading between
the possibilities, when my borders were irrevocably crossed.

This was the wildness each spiral feels as it twirls toward the edge.

The dome light clicked on when the door was opened,
off when the door was closed. That strobe light effect made my arms
look shorter and someone else's naked legs.

The serious students took turns. Sex was a subject they would never miss.
When I asked them to stop, they wouldn't. Light on, light off.
Tires trembled. The dangling car freshener rocked.

I wanted them to know me beautiful so I braced myself
against the arm rest and accepted one after another.
I was a length of pipe with the world passing through.
Parts of my body were cartooned on desktops that semester.

Behind the newspaper, my father's face. My mother made sure
that no one went hungry. Bearer of corn and potatoes,
she beat the rugs regularly and rolled each of her children tight as a pair
of socks. Her slacks were woven with strands of agony.
Winged creatures served her berries.

No one is beautiful except mothers. All little children raise their arms
to be held. Only violets and rhubarb are normal. A flash of teeth,
sickening roses, they remind me of the day I died.

I quit college and never told my parents what really happened. I just
let them believe whatever they wished. My whole life was a lie anyway.
Mom made up stories about my visiting a cousin in Ohio. In reality, they
signed me up with a social service agency. Then came the unsuccessful
attempts at being a "girl" in various households. As such, I was supposed
to work for my keep, with chores that ranged from babysitting for ten
children to ironing overflowing baskets of clothes to scrubbing a bathroom with bleach every day. I hated doing other people's work and was
eventually placed in a home for unwed mothers.

Boys called the place "Watermelon Hill" and drove by in their cars
yelling rude comments. I was not allowed contact with anyone except

my parents. On weekends when my folks brought me home for a visit, I would have to lie on the floor of the car, belly and all, so none of the neighbors would see me. All the shades in the house were drawn.

The "home" was everything I expected, complete with bars on the windows and dormitory cots. The nuns who ran the place spent mornings in chapel praying for our redemption. At the home, they gave us each a fake name made up of our real initials. My fake name was Laurel Taylor. We were not supposed to tell each other our real names. Mother Superior whisked up and down the halls, her black cloak flapping. We called her "the old bat" but everyone was afraid. She had the power to double—or triple—our chores, which included tasks like scrubbing the many steep wooden stairways, waxing the auditorium floors, and scraping garbage off one hundred plates.

They kept us very busy, because obviously the devil had taken hold of us at least once and, heaven knows, he might get us again. When I could get away with it, I stayed in bed as much as possible reading e.e. cummings, listening to Bob Dylan and writing page after page of poetry.

Babies were being born right and left. The girl in the cot on my left had twins. There was a rumor that she was going to keep them. Most girls placed their babies for adoption—gave them up. I wasn't sure about what to do.

I loved my baby even before I felt him move inside me. Having this baby was a good and important thing. In fact, it was the first important thing I had ever done. The chapel was a place to get away from everybody, and I ended up praying for guidance. When I realized that my baby was more important than my life, it became clear that I needed to give him up for adoption. Everything about me was a wreck. I couldn't offer him a decent future.

Time never moved so slowly. My favorite song was Paul Simon's "I am a rock, I am an island." I wondered if there was a way I could protect myself like that.

Finally, on a sunny day in July, the pains began. A taxi took me to the hospital. I can't remember if my mother was there or not. I think not, because I didn't want her there. There were women moaning and screaming in nearby rooms. I remember thinking how melodramatic they were. I never screamed or called out.

I had a baby boy and named him Jeffrey Philip Taylor. I thought it was a manly and sensitive name. He came a little early and was slightly jaundiced, but otherwise he was fine, they told me. I wanted to see him. The nurses refused. After a few days, we were both brought separately back to the home, and I made a fuss until they let me see him. I think I could have killed someone if they would have kept refusing my request. I'm not ordinarily fierce, but I was then.

I was put in a small white room with a white wooden rocking chair, and my baby was brought to me. He looked like a little angel, all sweet and precious. In the eerie white glow, I held him, rocked him, took off all his clothes and checked to make sure he was perfect. My mother had seen him through the glass at the hospital nursery. Just the sight of him changed her mind entirely, and she wanted me to keep him. But I kissed him good-bye. Honestly, I don't know how I could be so strong.

I made up a beautiful story about the baby's father for the social worker. I said he was Swedish, in case the baby turned out to be blonde (I had dark hair.) I claimed the father was a straight-A student, because I wanted to make sure the baby would go to college. I made it sound like the father and I had a long term, though ill-fated relationship.

I don't even remember signing the papers, but I must have. The social worker told me to go home and start my life all over again. I went home, told more lies and got an office job. I moved away from home as soon as I could. Being with my family and in that house was no good. I wanted to move on—to grow up or something.

I liked sharing an apartment with other girls, but they seemed so well adjusted, so "together." And I had this huge, ragged hole inside me. I cried for my baby every night—and for many years afterwards.

Making money became my top priority. I had to make enough to get out of town. I had to move on. California sounded good. My older brother was in the Navy, stationed in the San Francisco area. I wouldn't be totally alone.

To get enough money for an airplane ticket, I worked at a bank during the day and as a go-go dancer at night. As was the style in that era, I danced in a little cage. I wore a black leotard, net stockings, sleeveless sweater and a blonde wig. At the bank my uniform was a tailored green suit. It all fit perfectly with my double life, pretending to be myself but feeling like someone else inside.

With five hundred dollars in travelers' checks, I moved to San Francisco and got a room in a slightly run-down hotel on Bush Street. Every few days I had my room changed to a less expensive one. The front desk staff was very kind to me. I ate peanut butter sandwiches and apples and cried myself to sleep every night. Because of his duties, my brother rarely had time to see me. San Francisco wasn't any better. It was only lonelier.

After Saying Good-bye to My Baby I

When I was free in San Francisco
my plan of action was written in the sand
with one thin finger while the wind already
gathered to rework my fate.
The money saved from working two jobs
saved me from working for three months.
Too shy to talk, I took the bus to Sunset
where the unemployed fed pigeons
and wove gods-eyes and each day gave up
its ghostly hue by sliding into the sea.
Then back to my closet room with the bath
down the hall and the TV room where
I sat with the old and lost watching Dragnet reruns.
I was that girl I never knew and nobody wanted,
afraid of the hills, that they might tip over,
the pain of missing my baby pouring from my eyes.
At night in my bed I would hold him, my pillow.
I did not know how my life could go on
but I knew his would. Did he miss me?
Would he think me silly to kiss this?

Looking for something to hold on to.

My brother introduced me to his neighbor, Bill, who seemed nice but had his own problems. Bill's mother was manic-depressive, and years later he was diagnosed as chronically depressed. Bill and I became hippies together, dropping acid on the weekends and attending anti-war demonstrations in Berkeley, where we were treated to a whiff of tear gas. We spent long evenings at my place doing drugs and listening to the Doors, Cream and Big Brother & the Holding Company. Oddly conservative hippies, we both held full-time jobs during the week.

Bill and I decided to get married almost immediately. Actually, I think it was me who decided. We hadn't even known each other six weeks. My mother was thrilled and, I think, relieved that I'd finally found someone. I flew home, planned a quick wedding and went through with it, even though I had my doubts. We were married on March 16, 1968, the day of the My Lai massacre during the war in Vietnam. I flew back to Mountain View, California, with my new husband. I had a big diamond—an heirloom from his family—and hopes to match.

Things were never very good between us, although we did love each other after a fashion. We both had too many needs. My biggest need was to have a baby—one I could keep. We moved back to Minnesota because it was a better place to raise children. I got a job as a bank teller and soon was ecstatic to find myself pregnant. I couldn't wait to wear maternity clothes and start crocheting little booties and bonnets.

As was our summer custom, my mother and I went to visit my Great Aunt Lizzie, who lived on the family farm in Wisconsin. Great Aunt Pearl was there, too. "Life is so good," gushed Aunt Pearl, "My life has been so much fun . . . don't you wish you could just go back and do it all again?"

Aunt Lizzie leaned back in the rocker and answered, "I'd never want to live through all of that again."

I was shocked. I thought she had been happy. I made some comment about being happy now that I was finally going to have a baby. And Aunt Lizzie looked at me closely and said, "You shouldn't count on anything."

Maybe Aunt Lizzie was psychic or maybe it was fate, but I lost that baby at five months. The nurses said it was a blessing because something was wrong with the baby. But for me it was an unbearable curse. Sorting through all the soft little garments, my heart was worse than broken—it had died with the baby. Bill didn't know what to do with me, so he got me some anti-depressant medication. I remember not being able to get the childproof cap open and spilling the pills all over the tile floor, where they scattered like a shotgun blast. Then I sat on the bathroom floor watching the faucet, drop after drop.

Later that year, Michele was conceived. Everything went well, and I finally had my baby. She was my absolute joy. I poured my soul into her. Things were still not very good between Bill and me, but we both tried very hard. For the next several years we attended counseling. I started reading self-help books in addition to Dr. Spock.

Joel was born when Michele was three. The children were my life. They were enchanting, intelligent, gorgeous, wonderful. I became active in a parent-cooperative preschool program, church and neighborhood activities. But I still had that empty hole inside me caused by the loss of my first son. I knew then that other children couldn't fill his space. I wrote to the adoption agency periodically, and they sent me "non-identifying" information about him. It didn't really help, so I tried harder to forget about him.

Having replaced ourselves in the world, Bill and I decided not to give birth to any more children. But I wanted one more child. I began exploring international adoption, and Katie came into our family from Korea six months after we made application. She arrived on July 16, 1975, three days after Michele's fifth birthday, and the exact day of my first son's ninth birthday. I could never have planned for that to happen! I wondered if God was giving me some sort of sign.

Things seemed better, except for the increased stress of having two children in diapers and a weak marriage. I think what happened was that I changed and Bill didn't. At some point, maybe because of my social activities, new feminist friends or through some internal maturation process, I made a conscious decision to be happy. I decided not to be some wimpy woman at the mercy of whatever the fates dished out any longer. I was going to make a life for myself, no matter what. I knew if things stayed the way they were, I would die. I would just shrivel up and die. Bill and I broke up and got back together several times. Finally, I asked him to move out permanently.

The kids—especially Michele—hated me after the divorce. Michele was old enough to believe that the divorce was her fault. I worked very hard to reassure them all, but Joel stuttered for a long time and Katie wouldn't sleep through the night. Sometimes the tensions built up inside me and I was afraid I might hurt the kids. So I would lock myself in the bathroom until I felt stronger.

It was hard, being a single parent all those years. I knew it wasn't the worst thing that had ever happened to me, but it was right up there. But believe it or not, there was a bright side. When I made a decision, there was no one to argue with me.

Bill was always dependable with the child support payments, bless his heart. I located some part-time work at first, and then a series of jobs to make ends meet.

I wanted my kids to have as much love and nurturing as possible, and I didn't care where that love came from. I couldn't handle all their needs alone. Bill's emotional problems made it difficult for him to give affection. I found Katie a mentor family who had two adopted Korean kids. We are forever grateful for their love and companionship—and for Joel's "big brother" too, who boosted his self-confidence and encouraged him in outdoor activities.

After some research, I found a program that guided me through vocational testing, and I talked my way into the advertising industry, where I eventually got a job as a writer. How wonderful! Whoever thought that I could make a living doing what I loved best? What a kick that was—going to work every day thinking "Wow. I am a real writer!"

Ironically, I was suddenly popular with men. Some, though, wouldn't date me because I had children. As the old story goes, I kissed quite a lot of frogs before I found my prince. But find him I did. My best friend, my confidant, my strongest supporter, my soul mate, David.

PRIMER

Three years are long enough to learn
how to count, brush up and down,
get toilet trained.
Long enough to start thinking
Mister Rogers is dumb.
Three years are long enough
to outgrow Cinderella bedrooms,
animal slippers and nite lites.
For a smashed fingernail to grow back,
magic marker to wear off.
Long enough to lather peanut butter
between thick slices of loss—
a single parent, lonely enough
to learn from children the secrets
of horsies in marshmallow clouds,
the creamy center of a Twinkie.

Long enough to turn around and find
the man who finds horsies, windmills,
angels and unicorns
making peanut butter sandwiches
in your kitchen with your children
like he wants to marry you.

David and I gave the kids plenty of time to get used to the idea of our marriage. Michele was eleven, just the right age to question my every action. I thank my mother for taking her aside and telling her, "Your mother deserves to be happy. You want your mother to have someone who loves her, don't you?" Eventually, each of the children worked out their own individual arrangements for getting along with and learning to love David. Becka, David's daughter from a previous marriage, didn't live with us, but was an important part of the picture, too. There were certainly a lot of relationships to handle!

With David and me, the honeymoon lasted a long time. Even now, more than eleven years later, we're still crazy about each other. My new-found happiness was a boost to my creative capabilities—and I began to publish my poems in literary journals and magazines, while at the same time progressing in my advertising writing career.

The children grew from stage to stage, presenting an array of challenges along the way. All three were teenagers at the same time! David's daughter, Becka, was a brilliant student who eventually graduated from a private New York City college and now works as an editor in the publishing industry. Michele, also a brilliant student, achieved a graduate degree, travels extensively and is a teacher. Joel stumbled a bit in high school but then graduated with a high grade point average from a technical school and found a niche for himself in computer-aided design. Katie is still in college where she is blossoming, volunteering for Habitat for Humanity, making new friends and figuring out what her future holds.

Life was busy, and the pain of losing my first son faded into the background. The last update I requested and received was when he was fifteen. They said he was tall and handsome, a high school football star and avid hunter and fisherman. They said he liked to write stories. My feelings of loss never really healed, but sort of scabbed over.

One day in 1986, an art director I worked with told me about how she had recently found her birthson, due to the fairly recent changes in Minnesota adoption laws. It suddenly occurred to me, "Hey—I bet I could find my son."

As mentioned earlier, I had kept in touch with the adoption agency over the years, but it was never suggested that I could ever actually meet him.

When I decided to try, it all became unbelievably easy. After the obligatory face-to-face meeting with a social worker, the agency called the phone number they had on file. His family had moved, but just down the block. He had lived in the same small town his whole life.

His immediate response to the social worker's query was, "Sure! I've always wanted to meet her!"

We were at Katie's soccer banquet the night Tom, my first son, was due to call me for the first time. I could barely eat, and excused myself early to wait for the phone to ring. I sat at the edge of the bed.

His voice was unfamiliar, strange. He was a real person, a grown man. I don't think either of us could wait. We decided to meet the following Thursday, at a restaurant halfway between his college and the ad agency where I worked.

MOTHER AND SON REUNION

At 5 p.m. on November 13 we drove to Eduardo's Restaurante from separate cities.
He couldn't have looked more fragile, twenty years old in his red leather jacket.
On shaky Levi legs he stood to greet me for the first time.
Night mother, we meet at last, was what he didn't say.

Together we ate the whole meal of our lives on white plates,
full circles. Nothing he told me was new,
everything I told him was true as the slash of sun
that resolves the night.

My finger traced his nail's familiar shape—
two hands that, but for dark leaps of time,
should have known each other like gloves.
Together we broke crusts off bread,
watched the butter melt.

And what he didn't know was, this time
leaving him again, I wept for miles in the car,
for what is new in the sky's full promise—
what is alive beyond belief.

He looked beautiful and strangely familiar. He hugged me stiffly and I could tell that, like my dad, Tom didn't wear his heart on his sleeve. Sitting across the table from each other, neither of us could stop staring. The words poured out of both of us. He told me he was grateful to me for giving him such a good life. I was relieved that he hadn't felt unwanted or abandoned by me. I told him how I had held him and kissed him good-bye. He took my hand. He cried. We both cried. He showed me a picture of himself at seventeen as best man in his brother's wedding. I felt the deep loss of all the years I had missed.

After Tom and I met, there was a flurry of letters and phone calls and visits. The two of us took long walks around the lake. He is a middle child of three, just like me. His parents have similar personalities to my parents.

He told me that he had often thought and guessed things about me. Tom was always so caring and respectful of my feelings. He never even asked about his birth father, but I knew he must have been wondering. I finally worked up the courage to tell him about the rape.

Then I quickly added, "But I always thought of you as good—there was never anything bad about you."

His only response was to put his arm around my shoulders. We never talked about it again.

Tom was extremely interested in meeting his half siblings, especially Katie, with whom I think he felt a special connection, since she was adopted as well.

When I told my kids about him, it was difficult for them to adjust at first. I think they were afraid that they'd lose their places in the family. But it all smoothed over with time.

His parents were concerned, too, and I wrote them many letters to assure them that I wasn't going to insinuate myself into their family—that I respected them and thanked them for their good job in raising him. I was just so happy to know him. That big empty spot inside was finally filled.

The day David and I met Tom's parents, we pulled into their driveway on our big black motorcycle wearing leather jackets. I figured, "This is me. I might as well not play any games. Either they'll like me or they won't."

His parents were very polite, and served us iced tea on the couch. His mother had Tom's baby book and photo album on the coffee table for me. How thoughtful! She also gave me whatever photos I wanted from the album. There was a picture of him as a baby with his older brother. Pictures of him in grade school. I kept saying, "Oh, can I have this one? This one?"

"Of course," she replied.

I treasure those photos and wonder if I would have been as generous.

When I told my mom and dad that I had found Tom, they were very happy for me. They knew how much pain I had been through over the years. Dad and I had never really discussed any of what happened. Mom tended to be a lot more open about emotions, and we were starting to talk about it. Better late than never, I guess. Maybe it's because of time and maturity, but I'm closer to my parents now than I've ever been.

For a time after the reunion, Tom was all I could think about. I must have filled hundreds of pages with all my feelings. It was like a love affair of sorts. I could not get enough of him. I couldn't stop staring at him. He was my self, my core, mine, me. David was very patient with this sudden obsession of mine. I am forever grateful to him for that. Meeting my

A blended family.

son was the biggest joy, like winning the lottery or having your greatest wish come true.

Some part of me still misses everything I missed with Tom, and still feels that he should have been with me. Intellectually I know it was all for the best, but somehow my feelings don't quite match. There is a sort of bitterness or deep sadness. Writing this has taught me many things, and one is that I am still scarred by the whole experience. I thought I was over it, but I may never be.

Tom graduated from college with the intention of teaching social studies to junior high school kids and being an athletic coach. He married Becky, a girl from a nearby town. Mom and I were invited to Becky's bridal shower, and Mom, Dad, David and I attended the wedding. His family even gave me a corsage to wear! Mom and I both cried through the whole ceremony. She held my hand. At the reception, the photographer took a picture of Tom and me for their wedding album.

Tom is my only child who looks like me. He's the only one in his adopted family who likes to write. He's probably as stubborn as I am, too. The job market for teachers was tough. After a long search, summers spent laying sod and winters of substitute teaching, he never gave up looking for a job in his field. Instead he shifted gears, got his special education certification and is now happily teaching at a suburban high school and coaching football.

Tom and Becky share dinners, ballgames and other events with the family and us. Tom has a slow, easy sense of humor and warm nature, like his adoptive father—and my father. He can be very funny, especially when he doesn't know it. We love Becky, who is a beautiful, sensitive and talented young woman. She is a perfect partner for him and they're totally devoted to each other. She helps him remember my birthday and Mother's Day. She tells me that he loves and respects me and brags about me to his friends—things that he doesn't say to me. I think he loves me as a very special aunt. It's hard to put a label on the kind of love connected to this relationship.

After Saying Good-bye to My Baby II

These hills are friendly to my legs now,
not tipping me over, nor calling my bluff.
I am not afraid of the cable car this time,
but grab a handful of my husband's shirt
    as we career seemingly into the sea.
Too many times I have thought it safe
    to walk my dog to visit every tree,
    to examine too closely the past.
I have always known in which direction
    the sea lies, as I know the difference
        between dream and earthquake.
    I know my son now and he is tall,
    with my eyes and part of my pain.
    it is safe to kiss him now but touch
    is not much to fill up twenty years.
    This is just another city of flowers
and hoopla designed for the old and lost.
    I know my way around this time.

People tell me that I did a great job as a mother, but I sure can't take all the credit. My children are as well adjusted as any of us can hope for, and our connections together are very strong. They believe in themselves and are kind people. Bill and I did some things right together, and one of them was that we never made the children choose between us. We agreed that they deserve to love both of us. We both put their well being before our emotions and anger. We weren't perfect, but we always tried to work together for the benefit of the children.

All my children have moved out of the house now. That makes me happy and sad at the same time. After all, I didn't raise them to stay with me their whole lives, and now I can put more time into my writing life. Still, they've always been a huge part of who I am, and I miss them.

David and I have wonderful adventures together. We travel whenever possible—motorcycle trips to Wisconsin and trips to Europe, Mexico, and Jamaica. We flew to San Francisco this year when Michele received her master's degree from UC Berkeley. The Bay Area has changed almost as much as I have. I never believed my life would be this happy or full.

Tom and Becky have moved out of the city for now. He's in his glory at their little lake home—hunting, fishing and doing all the outdoor things he loves. So far, neither of them minds the commute. Becky is the Volunteer Coordinator at an English learning school for immigrants and refugees. I volunteer there, teaching a writing class—so she's my boss! She thinks that's pretty funny.

Once in awhile, Tom drops in at school after my class. Becky has told me that he would like to be closer with me. Of course, he'd never come right out and say that to me. But that's fine. I understand. His hugs have become a lot less stiff, and sometimes he walks up to me and kind of brushes my shoulder—which reminds me of the little nudges Dad used to give Mom when he passed her in the kitchen. Love is love, and it doesn't have to be shouted from the rooftops.

For years now, I've been dreaming about babies almost every night. They're not exactly recurring dreams, because each dream is different. I dream about brown babies, white babies, the baby powder smell of them, being pregnant, giving birth, dressing babies, finding babies in the jungle, rescuing babies from rubble, babies floating on clouds, kissing babies and simply holding them in my arms. A friend told me these dreams mean that I am helping babies move from one world into another. I don't know about that, but I do feel responsible. And I do love them so.

* * *

It's 1995 and Tom and Becky have announced that I am going to be a grandmother. This is a priceless gift. Another gift that was never expected. Does it make up for losing him at babyhood? Does finding him make up for twenty years of not knowing? The questions outweigh the answers.

NOT ANGRY ANY MORE

I was born whole, then spent some years disintegrating.
It is what I live with.
I built myself again, not without risk,
but with a soft voice for babies. I was valiant.
I survived. I decided to be happy.
I built a whole family.
I raised the children that were allowed to me.
I went on, because that is what people do.
We swallow the past and it becomes our blood and bones.
Everything we live is taken inside us like food—bitter and sweet—
to rest in quiet inside places. The loss is eternal.
It settles into another set of wrinkles across my forehead.
I am not angry any more. A little sad,
yes, and humbly grateful at the same time.
I put the sad in the back on a high shelf.

What we have lived is almost obsolete.
It is a recipe not for sharing.
The ingredients are rare, and that is good.
That recipe for dragon stew should be wrapped in white linen
and placed in an attic chest. It should molder in the dry heat of history.

* * *

Fourteen years later . . .

As DAVID SAYS, "Time is what keeps everything from happening all at once."
When I look back on these past years, it almost feels like everything did happen all at once. Tom and I continue to be very close emotionally, even though we don't see each other often. I am happy and grateful for the things I was able to do for him—things that were important to me. These include helping

him with his homework (I edited his thesis for his master's degree), buying him toys (for a number of years I gave him funny little toys at Christmas time), and getting him a puppy ("Bear," the white lab, went hunting with Tom before living his last happy days at Becky's parents' farm).

In late 1995 Tom and Becky rang our doorbell. We ushered them in out of the cold. They handed me a little package, which I opened. Inside were two little wooden hearts strung together with a length of ribbon. On one of the hearts were the words, "Grandmas are" and the other heart read "antique little girls."

"Grandma? Grandma? What does this mean?" I can be a little slow on the uptake.

They laughed and nodded. And that's how I found out I was going to be a grandma for the first time. I was thrilled. I think I may have jumped up and down. Becky put her arms around me.

"We don't want our kids to come over here and just sit at a dinner table. We want them to really know you," she said.

Allie was born the following June, and David and I were the first visitors at the hospital. She was the most beautiful baby—and now she's a beautiful teenager. Tom and Becky made sure that we were able to spend time with the baby. They've always been very generous that way. I cut back on my workload so I could baby sit more often. I knew how precious and fleeting that time was. I remember holding Allie on my shoulder and rocking her, taking in that sweet baby smell and thinking, "I couldn't have him, but look, look what I can have now." There is nothing more healing than a baby.

Nick was born on New Years' Day 1999. Another priceless gift. He was a happy little guy, always grinning, even though he had a tendency to spit up. I wore that "grandma badge" proudly—on both shoulders of my sweater. Don't tell Tom and Becky, but once when he was a baby and both grandkids were spending the night, I kept him up until midnight playing and laughing with him. Allie and Nick had many good times with us, and they both still remember going to the lake, Grandpa Dave "throwing" them in the water, getting to feed the giraffes at Como Zoo, picnics, holiday get-togethers and more. They do "really know" us.

Due to Tom's persistence, he did get a high school teaching job. In his field, social studies, Tom continues to do important work educating students—and the public—about the Holocaust. He has won awards for this work, and we are so proud of his efforts. Becky's job in the computer field has provided long-term stability for the family. They are solid parents, with a healthy sense of humor, which is important in child rearing.

I think I can safely say that my relationship with Tom has also been solid. When we first reunited, I expected that all of us—his family, my family, David's family—would all miraculously blend into one happy family. Yes, I was overly optimistic. I've always believed that no child can have too much love and I thought that I'd be welcomed as another love-giver. I continued to write newsy letters to Tom's mom and dad, including the yearly holiday missive, in which I would include news about Tom, Becky, and the kids. It was years later that Tom finally told me that his mom didn't exactly welcome any cards or letters from me. I was crushed and embarrassed. How could I have been so stupid? Tom and Becky hated to hurt me—I know that—but I do wish they had told me sooner. We have talked about it and now I understand that Tom needs to keep his birth family and his adoptive family separate. This, of course, is not ideal for me, but I could never bear losing him again, so I abide by his decision.

When Tom's adoptive dad died a few years ago, I agonized about whether or not I should attend the funeral. I decided to send a big bouquet of flowers and heartfelt sympathy cards instead. I think that was the best decision.

My dad, my mom, and my brother all died within five years of each other. At my dad's funeral, Allie had her arm around me the whole time. Tom and Becky have always been a huge comfort to me—in good times and difficult ones.

As I said in my original story, it's hard to put a name on the kind of love we have for each other. When we are all together, it is easier, sometimes, than being with the children I have raised. This may sound strange, but I think that ease is because there is a lack of the "baggage" that all children have with the parents who raised them. Especially now that Tom is getting older, we are more like friends than mother and son. With the grandchildren, though, we are one hundred percent Grandma Linda and Grandpa Dave.

Our other children have found their own ways, too.

Becka achieved her PhD and teaches at a university in Florida. She has a "labradoodle" named Sophie. We have very little contact with Becka—it's a long story—but the door is always open if she ever wants to rejoin the family.

Michele is married to Jorge, whom she met when she was in the Foreign Service and stationed in Lima, Peru. She now has her PhD in Second Language Acquisition and is a professor at a California university. Jorge is a professor in economics. Their son, Gabriel, loves soccer, math, and reading, not necessarily in that order. He is a definite leader—bright and loving. Joel and Rebecca got married on a beach in Mexico. Joel attended college at Minneapolis College of Art and Design and recently became a computer programmer for Twin Cities Public Television. Rebecca works full time, too, and in her spare time makes artistic cake creations for her many satisfied clients. They have a son, Evan, whose face still lights up when he sees me, and a daughter, Mikayla, who scrambles

Atari, a fortuitous gift.

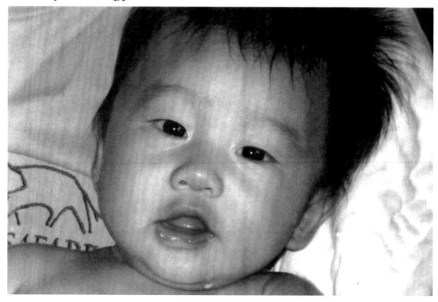

to keep up with Evan. Joel and family live only a couple of miles from us and the kids love to come visit Grandma and Grandpa. Daughter Katie met Calvin on a train in Portland, Oregon, and was immediately drawn to him. Katie seems to always manage to get what she wants. She is a true survivor. Katie and Calvin had a beautiful wedding on a rainy day in Portland and, after some time, welcomed their beloved son, Atari, into the world. Atari is a Japanese word that translates into "a fortuitous gift" or "winning the lottery."

I've been teaching more in recent years. I teach classes in poetry writing and publishing, among a few other things, including one-on-one sessions with a fascinating assortment of poets and writers.

David and I are closer than ever—especially when we travel in our little RV, which is only seventeen feet long. We joke about how polite we must be on those trips. The motorcycle follows us on a trailer. During the winter we head south and often visit Michele and family in California. Summers often find us in the Pacific Northwest. We plan to visit Europe again some day, but that will be an airplane trip.

I still dream about babies—feeding them, rescuing them from burning houses, finding food and clothes for them. Each dream contains something constant: My love for those babies.

Despite an uncertain economy, despite politics, war, and all the pain in the world, there is much to appreciate in life. I believe that, if we are lucky, we can choose how to receive what the universe hands us. We can either wallow in grief and loss or we can acknowledge the good and the bad and then move forward. Like Atari, I'm one of the lucky ones. I too have experienced many "a fortuitous gift."

Chapter Three

MARY

MY TWO BROTHERS, THREE SISTERS and I grew up in a house on the river in Central Minnesota. My parents had purchased sixty-three acres in that pastoral area, including a small cabin. The eight of us crammed ourselves into the cabin and somehow managed to live there. My dad kept adding on to the cabin until it was just about big enough for the family. The property was filled with hazel nut bushes, and we all pitched in to clear the land. It was just like "Little House on the Prairie." Except we had a boat, horses, and lawn mowers—the push variety. We shared in the chores and developed a strong work ethic. Our leisure time was spent swimming, water skiing and skating in the winter. It was definitely a clean and healthy way to grow up.

I started babysitting when I was about seven and I worked as a "Mom's helper" for ten cents an hour. In high school I got a housekeeping job working for a doctor. I wanted to be a policewoman but my grandma stepped in and said no.

"You'd see things no woman should ever see," she said.

My parents hadn't had much education and maybe that was why they encouraged all us kids—including the girls—to have something to "fall back on." My grandma agreed with them that nursing would be a good career for me. Dad said he would pay the two thousand dollars a year tuition, which included room, board, and books. So off I went to the relatively big town of St. Cloud and nursing school.

In those days we earned our keep by working eight hours a day on the nurses' floor. We worked as nurses' aids until we got our caps, which was after the first year. It was more on-the-job training than RN students have these days. Nurses now are more on par with the doctors. In those days we were supposed to kiss the ground they walked on.

I met Don during my last year of nursing school. He was operating an ambulance service in St. Cloud. We met at the hospital and flirted around a bit. When he called me for a date we started going out. Then I found out that he was married. With two kids. He told me they were separated, though, and I was naive enough to believe him.

My dad called Don "the red-headed bastard." He couldn't stand him because he was "used merchandise." We were strict Catholics and marriage was considered holy and forever. People who married divorced people were committing a mortal sin, which would damn them to hell. The more Dad disliked Don, the more I was attracted to him.

In September of 1965 I was living in Minneapolis and working at Golden Valley Hospital, now Courage Center. While driving up to St. Cloud for a sister's wedding, I felt sick and figured I had a touch of carsickness. It passed. Another sister got married that November. Mom had sewn the bridesmaid dresses for both weddings and she made mine the same size as last time.

I don't remember exactly when I realized I was pregnant. I knew I was having sex, but I just didn't get it. Birth control pills had become available, but Catholic girls didn't take the pill, or so I thought. And, I guess I figured if he was married he should know how to not get pregnant.

My parents' philosophy was, "If you do the crime, you do the time." The guilt was one of the reasons why I didn't tell them. I covered up my condition for as long as I could, but when I started showing, I had to quit my job. Don let me stay at his friend's lake cabin near St. Cloud. I lived there alone from December 1965 until May 1966. It was just me and Mitzi, my little Scottie dog. I had been saving money for a purebred Scottie and I sure did need a friend. She was my loving pal. Interestingly, Mitzi didn't seem to like Don any better than my father did.

Nobody knew about my being pregnant except Don. I got a post office box and wrote letters home, making up pleasant stories about my life. Don arranged for me to go to a doctor and to have the baby in Brainerd, where nobody knew me. He said he was going to marry me. His divorce was final in January 1966. There was a six month waiting period for remarriage. I'm a little foggy on this but I think he said he wouldn't marry me if I kept the baby.

On Saturday, April 23, 1966, I woke up in labor. Don drove me to Brainerd and dropped me off at the hospital. I didn't see him again until he picked me up to bring me home. The hospital was super busy. They put me in a bed in the hall with a screen around it. I ignored the whole experience until my water broke. Then I was terribly embarrassed, thinking I had wet the bed. I remember a mask being lowered onto my face. The baby was born late that night. They whisked the baby away and didn't want me to see her. I had a fit and wanted them to unwrap her so I could count fingers and toes. I finally did get to see her—on the day I left the hospital. She was all swaddled up and sleeping peacefully. It's hard to remember a clear picture of her face through my tears. I turned away and left.

I know that they gave me about the worst episiotomy ever. I couldn't walk, couldn't sit. In constant pain, I was supposed to soak my bottom four times a day. Since there was only a shower at the cabin and no tub, I had to use a basin. I can still see myself, alone, with my butt in the basin, crying, with Mitzi, powerless to help, at my side.

According to the records I received much later from Catholic Charities, I had called them in June 1966 "out of control with grief." I don't remember any of it. I blanked it out, just like I was supposed to. It's all jumbled in my memory. I must have contacted Catholic Charities about the adoption. They sent a social worker to Brainerd to pick up the baby. I think she went to her parents on May 19. It could have been sooner but the dad was away on business and the mom didn't want to make the trip alone.

In August of 1966 I married Don. My parents said my marriage would never last, but I was going to prove them wrong. We moved to Seattle in March of 1967. I worked at Group Health Hospital in the nursery, of all places. It was very hard to be with other people's babies and it was terrible when the premature infant I nursed for six weeks died on me. That's when I transferred out and began working in OR. I wore a lot of different hats during the ensuing twelve years I worked at that hospital.

Patti was born in February of 1969. I needed a baby and was determined to have one, no matter what. The marriage was rocky at best. Don had a bad habit of picking up women. When I finally had enough, I packed up five-year-old Patti and left. Don and I divorced in 1976.

Patti and I made a good life for ourselves in Kirkland, Washington. I went back to school and studied nursing anesthesia, which gave me a better salary to support my little family. Don did pay some child support, which helped.

I remained in contact with Don's first two kids, especially Bill who came to live with us when he was fifteen. When we separated, Bill stayed with Don but kept touch with me. My stepson married in 1980 and moved to Arizona. Sadly, he died of kidney cancer in 1995. I loved him so much. After his death, his widow, Tara, asked me about "the baby boy" I had placed for adoption. During my marriage, my first baby was always the "elephant in the room." It was never talked about. I told Tara the story and she sympathized with me and encouraged me to tell Patti she had a sister.

Patti had gotten married in November 1994. By March of 1998 she and her husband, Ted, were undergoing infertility testing. I drove her to some of the doctor appointments. During one trip she started talking about looking into adoption. I had been trying to find a way to tell her about her sister for three years at that point. On the way home from the doctor's office, it all finally came out. I told her the whole sordid story. We were both in tears when I dropped her off at her house. By the time I got home, four miles away, the phone was ringing. Patti had already called Catholic Charities and requested search paperwork for me. She was determined to find her sister.

I was terrified. I didn't think I had the right to find my first daughter. How would she feel about me?

"Did you fill out the papers yet?" Patti kept asking. And, "Did you hear anything yet?"

I kept saying no, but truth was, I didn't have the courage to even fill them out. Let alone mail them. It took me a good three weeks to accomplish that.

Before long I got a phone call.

"Something will be happening soon," the social worker said. "Your daughter has been in contact and has recently updated her file."

Wow, I thought. Maybe I'll see her on her birthday. But her birthday came and went. The social worker told me that when she called, my first daughter's phone just rang and rang. I finally asked her to send a letter instead. The letter found its way to her. The phone number had been an old one and the postal forwarding service was close to expiration—it seemed that we were meant to find each other.

I was filled with anxiety. Our first exchange of information was through Catholic Charities. They told me her name—Kathleen Ellen. I had named her Teri Lynn. We talked on the phone for the first time on June 17, 1998. I felt like I might burst with emotion. She had four little children, the youngest just a baby. We both wanted desperately to meet as soon as possible. But I had a job in Washington and she lived in Minnesota.

My mom's eightieth birthday was coming up, and I arranged to fly back to Minnesota early. I would stay with my sister in the Twin Cities before driving up north. Kathy and I planned to meet at the Mall of America, but when I got off the plane, there, standing next to my sister, was Kathy.

"There was no way my birthmom would come to Minnesota and I wouldn't be there," Kathy said.

I remembered later, though, despite what she had said, how she kept the baby in front of her all the time, as if to establish a distance between us. I was much too excited to notice much at that point. We all went to one of the airport restaurants. I had brought along photos of Patti, Ted, and even Don.

We met at the mall the next day and then her house. I saw her wedding pictures and met the children, but they didn't seem like my grandchildren. They were strangers. And I knew Kathy was my child but I didn't know her, either. It was all very confusing.

Before my drive to St. Cloud for the birthday party, I called my siblings and told them about meeting Kathy, asking them to not tell my parents because I wanted to do that in person.

"There is something I'd like to share with you both," I told Mom and Dad when we were alone. "I'd like you to be happy for me, but I'd understand if you didn't want to be part of it." Then I told them.

"How did you keep this from us?" was Mom's response.

Dad said, "That red-headed bastard has even more to answer for!"

Patti was flying up from Washington for the party and my sisters talked dad into letting Kathy come to the party, too.

Kathy and Patti seemed to fall in love with each other. While growing up, Patti used to say, "All I want is a big sister." Not a baby sister, but a big sister. And now she had one.

After the party, which went remarkably well, I had to go home to Washington to work, but Patti stayed on for a week. Patti and Kathy spent every waking moment doing sister-type things. Making up for lost time.

The girls became very close. My retirement party was in October 1998. Patti made a plan to have Kathy at the party. Kathy showed a video of her growing up years and by the end of it, everyone was crying into their napkins.

The three of us went to Mazatlan, Mexico for a vacation in the dead of winter 1999. It was on the warm sandy beach that Patti announced that she and Ted were moving to Minnesota to be close to Kathy. I was not surprised.

During the planning of Patti's going-away party, I asked her, "What's your favorite food?"

"Pickles and ice cream!"

That was how she told me about her and Ted's pregnancy. Finally! I was so happy for them. Little Kari was born later that year.

There were several factors that helped me decide to move back to Minnesota. My parents were getting old. My two daughters were there. And now Kari. I decided not to be separated from my family any longer.

I moved back to Minnesota in March of 2000. I bought a house and put down roots and everything was wonderful. Our reunion and family life was a fairy tale of happiness. Patti and Kathy shared childcare duties and it was really one big happy family

After all the problems getting pregnant with her first, Patti and Ted had two more babies, no problem. Mandi and then James. Patti and Kathy continued to be as close as any sisters could be. I was thrilled for all of us.

In 2008, a few uncomfortable things started happening. I knew that Patti was having some marital problems and I knew she was confiding in Kathy. But Kathy didn't seem to take Patti seriously.

"Just have a glass of wine and enjoy the sex," she told Patti.

I don't know the exact scope of the problems, but I was surprised that Kathy wasn't more supportive, given how close the two girls had become.

I had been planning for my mom's ninetieth birthday party, telling all her grandkids and great-grandkids to "save the date." I didn't get a confirmation from Kathy, so I asked her about it.

"Oh, I'm not going to be there," Kathy said.

"Why?"

"My dad has a week in Montana planned."

I was shocked and hurt. "But you've known about this so far in advance! It's sad that you don't think it's important."

Kathy responded, "But I've already met all your relatives. What do you want me to do about it?"

"Well," I said, "it would have been nice if you'd have told your parents so they wouldn't double book you."

That's when the separation started. Patti, Kathy, and I had been seeing each other at least weekly, sometimes more often. Our times together started being fewer and farther between.

Patti's husband, Ted, had a growing problem with alcohol, often drinking until he passed out. In June 2009 he called her, obviously drunk.

"I'm sorry I'm not the man you deserve," Ted said, "and not the father my kids deserve."

Ted wouldn't say where he was calling from. Patti, worried, tried a few phone numbers and then called Kathy. It turns out that Ted was in Kathy's basement, drinking or passed out. After that phone call, Patti became frightened about what Ted might do. She managed to get rid of all Ted's guns. He had several for hunting.

When Patti asked Ted for a separation, Kathy's comment was, "How could you do something like this without talking to me?"

The strange disconnect continued. There was something going on between Kathy and Ted. Was she giving him alcohol, even though she knew it was a problem?

Ted was due to move out of the house in two weeks. Patti and the children had tried to share a living space but it just wasn't working.

One day while Patti was at work, Ted sent Kathy a text message: "if there's a god i'll be with dad tonight." His father had died twelve years earlier.

Panicked, Kathy called me and said, "Where's Ted?"

I was out of town at my Mom's because she'd been sick. "Check at home. What's going on?"

Kathy hung up and called back later. "I found him at his house with a gun to his head and the police are on their way."

I immediately called Patti to let her know. I told her to hurry home. The little girls were due home from school. She said she was on her way.

I called Kathy and said, "Quick, go meet the girls at the bus stop so they don't see any of this.

"I can't," said Kathy. "I have to stay here with him."

Why did Kathy have to stay there with Ted? My drive home contained a flurry of emotional phone calls. When I got to Patti's house, the police had the whole block cordoned off. Since Ted had a gun, it was uncertain how he'd use it. After a while, the police were able to convince Ted to come out of the house, and they disarmed him.

As the police handcuffed Ted and started walking him away, Kathy stood watching.

I can only imagine what she was feeling. Her brother had committed suicide at the age of twenty-one, suddenly and without any warning signs.

Patti filed for an Order for Protection, and the judge decreed that Ted could have no face-to-face contact with Patti and that he could have only supervised visits with the children. The court ordered Ted to undergo treatment for his alcoholism. He became sober for a time, but not for long.

Kathy was completely against the order for protection. She said that Patti was keeping him from his kids, and that's all he lived for. It was all very strange. It was like Kathy was adopting Ted or something. Maybe she was trying to help Ted like she couldn't help her brother. Kathy moved Ted into her house, then found a condo for him to rent. She furnished the condo, shopped and cooked for him. Kathy wanted to supervise his visits with the children, but Patti said no, because Ted had been drinking with Kathy and she didn't want her kids to be around his drinking and, god forbid, his guns.

I became the supervisor for Ted's visits. It was weird how Kathy was always there—hanging his shower curtain, making a sandwich for herself as if it were her kitchen, and other things.

After a visit I supervised on Thanksgiving weekend 2009, there were no more get-togethers with Kathy, no more cards or phone calls.

In May of 2010, Patti was trying to finalize their child support situation. The court date was set for July, but Ted, with Kathy's help, kept getting the date delayed. She was also helping Ted try to find out how much money Patti had stashed away. I couldn't understand why Kathy had insinuated herself into Patti and Ted's financial disputes.

The following October, Kathy "unfriended" me on Facebook. I sent her a message saying I didn't understand.

She wrote, "You kept their divorce from being finalized."

What? I was wondering what Ted had been telling her.

"What are you talking about?" I wrote.

"You have abandoned me," wrote Kathy. "I didn't feel this as an infant but I feel it now."

"I never abandoned you. When I couldn't care for you, arrangements were made for your care," I wrote. "You're walking away from me now."

Kathy's response was, "I can answer those things but not now."

That's it. Our last contact. I kept sending birthday cards and presents to Kathy and her children, with never a response.

In April 2011 I made my last gasp attempt. I embroidered a heart-shaped pillow for her birthday. I brought it to her house and knocked at the door. Kathy answered the door and stood in the doorway, looking at me. When I tried to hand her the present she stepped back. Finally I slid the sad little package across the floor to her. We stared at each other, I turned and walked to my car.

"Have a great birthday," I said.

When Kathy's daughter's high school graduation party invitation came in the mail, I thought Kathy might want to reconcile. At the graduation, Kathy and the two older girls kept their distance from me. The two younger ones seemed happy to see me.

Shortly thereafter I sent Kathy an email thanking her for the party invitation and suggesting that we have lunch. There was no response. How hard is it to hit the reply key and respond? Maybe the invitation had come because Kathy had just wanted another graduation present for her daughter. I felt confused, hurt and helpless.

I waited about six weeks and tried again. "I guess your silence is my response."

There was no response. There was no contact between Kathy and Patti either, which is doubly sad. To go from communicating many times a week to no communication was very difficult for Patti, who shared many of my feelings. I had no idea why all of this happened and why Kathy cut off contact with me. When I have a problem with a person I talk about it. I did not know what to do with this silence. The whole thing turned from a fairy tale into a nightmare.

At the end of August 2011, I sent another email to Kathy, letting her know how painful these years have been for me and that I have started seeing a counselor to help me work through things.

Kathy wrote back, "These letters are more harmful than helpful. Would you mind if we saw a counselor? This name-calling is harmful."

I didn't think that we were doing any name-calling. We hadn't even had contact with each other. But I told her that I would see any counselor of her choice at any time. And that I would wait to hear from her and not initiate any more contact.

That was months ago. I really don't know how and if I can reach out again. Patti's children and Kathy's children see each other when Patti's kids visit with Ted. Other than that, all those precious ties have been severed.

Since 2002 I have moderated an online reunited birthmothers group called "Sunflower First Moms." I have heard every kind of reunion story there is. Because mine was such a happy story, it's particularly difficult to tell it now. Everything is so out of my control.

The main reason I am telling my story is so people know that reunions can go all sorts of ways. It's a shared responsibility. From my point of view, Kathy seems to lack empathy. She probably has an entirely differ-ent reality. I'm not saying that I'm right or that she's right. It's just a tragedy, what has happened to my family.

I wonder what Kathy has told her children about me and whether I'll ever see any of them. I wonder if I can ever trust her again. I wonder if I'll even get the chance.

Chapter Four

KARLA

ONLY CHILD, LONELY CHILD. That was me growing up. In 1939 when I was three, my mother divorced my father and sent me to live with her parents on the family farm in northern Minnesota. I don't think Mom ever knew how abandoned and unloved I would feel—as a little kid and for the rest of my life. My mother had her own problems. I didn't realize it then but she was an alcoholic, destined to marry an unfortunate succession of alcoholic and abusive husbands.

I only remember nighttime things about my father. I remember watching his big white shoes stepping heavily across our linoleum floor, glowing in the dark. And I remember one night when he was drinking, and hitting Mom, I protested and he pushed me out the window. I fell onto the fire escape and huddled there for hours, afraid to go back into the apartment. It was cold. I remember thinking, "Why doesn't Mom fight back?" But she never did.

Living with my grandparents was hard work. My grandparents were very poor and very strict. Their motto was, "If you don't work, you don't eat." Even as a little child I had to feed the chickens, peel potatoes, scrub my grandfather's dirty socks and more. I really didn't mind the work. I think the highly structured environment was good for me. I knew what to expect and I knew my limits.

My grandparents didn't own a tractor, let alone a car. Gramp had built the two-room log cabin with his own hands, and farmed with a team of horses. They were pious Methodists who believed "Spare the rod, spoil the child."

Every day I'd get up at 4:00 a.m., do barn chores and house chores, then walk three and a half miles to Spring Creek School. It was a one-room schoolhouse. My teacher, Mrs. Hutchinson, taught the eight-student class that spanned five grades.

After school, I'd help prepare the evening meal. When the crops were bad, we ate mush—a mixture of flour and milk. Gram tried to fix it all sorts of different ways, sometimes mixing potatoes into it. After supper, we listened to the radio for a while, read the bible, then went to bed.

We got drinking water from the river and kept it in a pail. We tried to save the rainwater for our hair. Milk and cheese came from our two cows. I still remember the day one of them died. It was terrible. When you have only two cows and you lose one of them, that's traumatic.

Perishable food was kept in crocks sunken into the cool ground and tightly covered, so snakes wouldn't get in. On winter nights we had to keep an all-night vigil at the wood stove so the water in the house wouldn't freeze.

Gram washed our clothes in two tin tubs. She'd boil the clothes first on the stove and then scrub them on the washboard. Sometimes her knuckles would bleed. She never complained.

On weekends, Gram instructed me in sewing and baking, and sometimes Gramp would take me fishing. I loved going fishing with Gramp, watching the sun sparkle on the river. It made me feel special, being together with him. Peaceful, too.

Every so often my mother showed up at the farmhouse door, wanting me to come live with her again. So off I'd go, with my little suitcase and big expectations. My hopes for a happy family never lasted long though, and I'd usually be back with my grandparents within a few weeks. Mom said it was because her job as a waitress took up so much time. I knew that she had boyfriends too, and was "sick" a lot.

I saw Gram and Gramp as perfect people. I still do. They were my protectors. I always tried hard to please them. I know my grandparents loved me in their own way, but I couldn't seem to overcome the empty feeling of loneliness I always carried around inside me. At night in my bed, I watched the stars through my window and dreamed about growing up, marrying someone who really loved me and having twelve rosy-cheeked children. We'd be a real family. I could almost see their faces.

My mother remarried in 1949 when I was thirteen. She sent a letter to Gram wondering if I wanted to come live with them in Minneapolis. I was ecstatic. Finally, we could be a family! I begged Gram to let me go. I think she knew it wasn't a good idea, but she helped me pack and paid my train fare. The neighbor drove me to the train station. I can still remember Gram and Gramp, looking so sad at the rickety back door of the farmhouse.

I guess Mom didn't remember that I was coming. I ended up waiting on the apartment steps until the bars closed. I'll never forget the look of shock on my stepfather's face when he saw me there. She hadn't even told him that I existed! That made two surprises, because I couldn't help but notice that my mother was pregnant. I felt like Mom had betrayed me, and I'll bet my stepfather felt betrayed, too.

Ours was not a happy household. There was a lot of yelling and fighting. There was mental and physical abuse and of course, alcoholism. I remember books being thrown, dishes being broken, a lot of swearing and feeling like I wanted to disappear. My grandparents had taught me about God and right from wrong, but there was no religion in my mother's house. I was so confused.

At school I fell in with a rowdy crowd, which by today's standards would be considered tame. I chose them as friends because they were the only kids who accepted me. We'd go to the drive-ins for Cokes and fries, and to the park where Jerry played guitar and we all sang along. Some of the kids smoked cigarettes, but not me. I was always at someone else's place or hanging out somewhere. Because I was so embarrassed by my family, I never brought a friend to my house.

When my little half sister Leah was born, I became the instant built-in baby-sitter. More than a baby-sitter, actually—I was more like her mother. It felt good to me, doing something important like taking care of a baby. And little children don't hurt you like adults can. But I had to take her with me wherever I went, and that was a pain. If only my mother had kept a better eye on things, she would have realized this was too much responsibility for a fourteen-year-old.

Once when Leah was still a baby, I stayed out all night with my friends from school. It was completely innocent. We just listened to records and had Cokes. But when I came home, Mom shouted at me about what a tramp I was and dragged me to the doctor to be "checked." I don't think she believed the doctor when he assured her my virginity was still intact. It may sound strange, but I still feel hurt that she didn't believe me. And that doctor visit was so embarrassing!

At fifteen, I started running away from home. I just had to get out of there. I felt like if I stayed in that sick place any longer I would explode. But they always found me and brought me back. My stepfather didn't have a clue about how to handle kids, let alone a teenager. My mother kept telling me, "If you don't do something right, you'll never amount to anything!" But instead of trying harder, I began losing what little confidence I had in myself.

In spite of my outward behavior, I still believed in the strict morals my grandparents had taught me. I was truly appalled when I found out about "bad girls." Although sex was an unmentionable subject, especially in my grandparents' home, I firmly believed that to have sex before marriage was a terrible sin.

On the farm, whenever I'd been scolded or felt unhappy, I had my own special "magic" place—a clearing in the woods where the trees grew together at the top like a church steeple. I would stand there, on top of a stump, and sing "Mockingbird Hill" as loud as I could. The leaves moved and rustled against each other as if they were applauding, and I bowed to my appreciative audience, yearning to become a real singer someday.

There was no place to sing at my Mom's house. I couldn't stand my life—never knowing who would be drunk or who would throw things. Maybe I kept running away to get attention. Negative attention was better than nothing. My mom and stepdad started turning me in to the police, and I found myself in the juvenile court system.

I knew I wasn't a bad girl, but I felt like I couldn't figure out anything, except that everything was my fault. The one thing that made sense to me was when a judge said, "This girl doesn't belong here. And the next time you people are back here in court, you will be the ones that I'll punish."

At seventeen, I met Charlie, who was in the Navy. I fell for him like a ton of bricks—his brown curly hair, cute smile, and handsome uniform.

I felt extremely guilty about having sex with him, but since I gave him my virginity I knew I had to give him my hand.

We got married that same year—1953. It was a small, quiet wedding. We moved in with his brother in Michigan. It was hard, having to live with another couple. Charlie was always nice enough but he never wanted to get a job. My grandparents brought me up to believe that a husband was supposed to support his wife. I wanted to make something of my marriage, but Charlie just couldn't change.

I divorced him when I was eighteen, and moved back to Minneapolis, where I worked as a waitress during the day, and as a ballroom dance teacher at night. The dance school trained me. My real father had been a musician so maybe that's why I've always loved music. I shared a little apartment with another girl and life seemed tolerable, even happy sometimes. I even got myself a job as a cocktail lounge singer, which was a dream come true.

Then Tim came into my life, with his flashing smile and coal-black eyes. Tim was wonderful, loved to dance and drank only 7-Up. The only problem was, Tim was still married. But his wife didn't understand him, and they were separated. Yes, I was pretty dumb.

Believing he'd soon be free, I let myself get carried away, and in 1955, at the ripe old age of nineteen, I found myself pregnant and unmarried. What's worse, when Tim's wife found out he was seeing somebody she wanted him back. He was like a ping pong ball between the two of us. He said it was the pressure that started him drinking again. I didn't even know he had a drinking problem. I didn't want any more drunks in my life but I was stuck. I loved him.

I continued singing as long as I could—mostly one-nighters. One of the bands I sang with just wanted me to just sit there on stage and look pretty. I joined a trio and went country which was more stable than pop. Our gigs were all over the five-state area, from Bismarck, North Dakota, to Brainerd, Minnesota, to Iowa City, Iowa.

I couldn't sing or work in public after I started showing, so I babysat for neighbors until Monica was born. When I looked into her sweet little face for the first time, I thought to myself, "That's it for me. Now I will always be one of those 'bad' girls." But I loved my baby daughter fiercely, and was determined to escape from my past.

I scraped up enough money to take a train to Los Angeles, California, where I found a job in a pastrami shop, got a cheap apartment and a baby-sitter for Monica. I never let Tim know where we were because I knew I had to get over him.

For several months everything was settled and peaceful. Then another uniform entered the picture. At first I thought Rollie was a police officer, but it turned out he was just a security guard. We had a lot in common, with both of us being Norwegian and from the Midwest. He took me out to dinner and dancing, and never seemed to drink too much. It was good to have a little fun again.

One day I got a letter from Mom. Because of a big fight with my stepdad, she wanted to bring my half sister Leah to Los Angeles and stay with me. What could I do? I gave up my apartment, rented a bigger one that I couldn't afford, and tried to prepare myself for living with Mom again.

Mom and Leah were only with me a couple of weeks before Mom patched things up with my stepdad. I should never have let it happen, but Mom talked me into letting her take Monica home with her. I was so dumb. I knew my finances were a mess, and figured I'd work two jobs, get ahead and then send for Monica. Rollie thought it was a good idea and I went along with it.

After Mom left with Leah and my daughter, Rollie and I moved in together. As my luck would have it, Rollie had a drinking problem too. I ignored it for as long as I could. But I was starting to feel lost and lonely again, and I missed my baby terribly. I remember watching the neighborhood children out the window. The sound of them playing and laughing became louder and louder, until it was a roaring in my head. At that point something snapped, and I knew I just had to have my sweet daughter back with me.

Rollie was hurt when I left. He believed I was going back to Tim, no matter how I tried to convince him otherwise. Ignoring Rollie's protests, I sold everything I owned, which was barely enough for the round trip train fare to Minnesota.

I arrived in Minneapolis only to discover that Tim's mother had taken Monica to Texas. My own mother hadn't even let me know! Barely able to think, I exchanged my return ticket to California for a ticket to Houston.

I'm not a brave person, and I don't know how I had the guts, but I made the cab wait in front of Tim's mother's house, ran in, grabbed my baby, and left in the same cab. Tim's mother was so shocked, she didn't even protest. It was pretty dramatic, like something out of a soap opera. But I had my Monica, and I promised my little girl we'd never be separated again.

Back in Minneapolis, totally broke, I called Rollie and asked him for money for Monica and me to come home. "Don't bother coming back," was what he told me.

He assumed I had gotten together with Tim and it hadn't worked out. I could tell by his voice that Rollie had been drinking. But I didn't think I had a choice. I had to go back to California because I was pregnant with Rollie's baby. I thought I belonged with him, and was sure I could convince Rollie to take me back. We could get married and be a family.

Isn't it funny that, after everything, I had such a positive attitude? Like Mary Poppins, I always believed in a bright side. Maybe that's part of what makes me a survivor.

I begged Mom for some money to get to California, and she finally gave it to me. Nobody knew I was pregnant. Not Mom, not my grandparents . . . nobody except Rollie, who was cold as stone and flatly refused to see me. I was more lonely than ever, depressed and scared. I cried all the time. I couldn't understand how Rollie could turn his back on me.

Feeling desperate, I went to the Red Cross in Los Angeles. They were kind and helped me find a baby-sitter for Monica so I could work. They also put me in touch with a California adoption agency. The agency social worker explained adoption and offered to help me find a place to live and pay my medical bills if only I would agree to the unselfish act of giving up my child to a loving couple unable to have children.

According to the social worker, the only clients this agency had were loving, well established and able to give my baby everything I couldn't. It was made clear to me that this would be in the best interest of my unborn child. Miserable, I agreed. I couldn't see any other choice.

Shortly after my signing up with the agency, Monica and I moved in with a rich family in Sherman Oaks. I cooked, cleaned and took care of their children in return for a room that I could occasionally escape to. I was so lonely and sad, knowing there was much more sadness up ahead. I felt like I was drowning, but I had to put on a happy face for my employer and for Monica. I'm sure that kind of stress takes its toll on a person's health.

I became very sick with the Asian flu, had a high fever and drifted in and out of consciousness. Weak as a kitten, I went into labor two weeks early. The lady I worked for took me to the hospital and left me there. She was nice enough to take care of Monica while I was gone. It was a very long and difficult delivery and a breach birth. I was pretty much out of it, but after I woke up I begged to see my new baby girl. The nurses weren't going to allow it at first, but they couldn't calm me any other way. I had to know she was perfect so she'd be sure to get a good family.

My baby and I spent little pieces of time together each day. I named her Constance. I knew this was my only chance to ever talk to her so I told her, "Always be a good girl, honey. And remember, Mommy will love you forever."

One day the adoption agency social worker walked in while I was holding Constance. She seemed very angry. I'll never forget the feeling of her pulling my baby out of my arms.

When the social worker handed me the papers, I couldn't see where to sign my name because of the tears. It was hard to breathe. There was such a deep pain inside me. But I signed, feeling great pressure to keep my word to the adoption agency. I was never told I could change my mind. I was never told there might have been a way for me to keep Constance, such as help from welfare. I was made to understand that once I signed the papers, that was it. No waiting period. No going back.

None of my family and friends knew I had given birth to another daughter, so I had no support system at all. The sadness, sickness and loneliness had left me thin and pale. It was all I could do to take care of Monica.

For the next month I was in deep depression. I didn't want to see anyone, but when Monica's father, Tim, called from out of the blue, I agreed to have dinner with him. He told me he was finally divorced, had quit drinking and had come to California to tell me that now we could get married. I thought, "Oh, why couldn't this have happened a month ago?"

I told Tim about the baby, and he was sympathetic. It was nice being with someone who understood me.

Tim and I did marry. I began looking for information about my baby when Constance was about three months old. The adoption agency acted as if I didn't exist.

The following year I gave birth to another daughter, who only lived two days because her lungs weren't fully developed. We moved back to Minnesota, and I became pregnant again, but there was something wrong and the doctors had to abort my baby son. They told me I could never have any more children. I figured this was my punishment for all my sins.

Every few months I wrote to California, asking the agency for news about Constance. Those first letters were never answered.

During our seven years of marriage, Tim fought an uphill battle with his alcoholism. Our relationship became more and more strained. Finally I gave up and we divorced.

I tried again to find Constance, but the adoption agency still would not return my phone calls. When I finally did get to talk to a real person, I was refused any information. I dedicated myself to raising Monica and trying to keep my head on straight. Monica was a beautiful child with a sweet disposition and was very talented musically. I worked hard to make sure I could always afford her dance lessons, which she loved.

In 1963, while working as a waitress in a bar, I met Len, the bar manager. We dated for several months, and he appeared to be a hard worker and very mature. It was only after we were married that I discovered that he had problems not only with alcohol, but also with other women.

Amazingly, I became pregnant almost right away. Len became physically and verbally abusive. He didn't think I was "his" anymore if I was carrying a child. I think it had something to do with the hatred he had for his mother that was transferred to me. I told Len we had to go to marriage counseling but he said, "No way. I'm not telling any stranger about my private life."

Nevertheless, I had two children with him. Theresa and John were both "miracle babies," and both premature. Theresa weighed less than two pounds, John just over three pounds. God blessed me with the gift of having them, and they both overcame all the physical problems associated with early birth.

After seven years of marriage to Len, I decided I didn't want my kids to live like this, and didn't want them to see Len hit me anymore. Above all, I didn't want to be like Mom and not fight back. Hence, my third divorce.

I stepped up my efforts to find Constance. In my mind, if I could just find her, I would feel whole again. As I mentioned, during the first ten years of searching, my requests to the agency were ignored. I went to libraries and looked for clues from all over the country. During the second decade the agency began answering my letters but told me no information was available. I kept searching through any records I could find.

I searched like a woman possessed during the third ten years. For some reason, the urge to find her became stronger and stronger until it was the biggest thing in my life. Now I was writing weekly letters to the agency, pleading for information. Every lunch hour, every evening, every weekend found me in the library checking all sorts of records, including California telephone books.

My other three children were growing up, and I tried hard to take care of their needs. But every night when I went to bed, when everything was quiet, I felt like my lost baby was calling out for me.

The Mormon library was very helpful to me in searching the birth records of Los Angeles County. When I knew Constance was old enough to be married, I began checking Los Angeles County marriage records.

During this period of time, I changed the way I was praying. Instead of praying so hard that God would let me find her, I began praying for her—for her soul and her health.

Finally in 1990, I located someone who I thought might be my daughter. Something inside me told me this was my daughter. Still, I could barely let myself believe it. After wasting so much time looking in other parts of the country, there she was in Los Angeles—right where I had left her!

I gathered every bit of information I could about her, including address and phone number. But something stopped me from making the call. I couldn't do it. I couldn't face the possibility of being rejected again. It took me three months to get up the courage to dial that long distance phone number. I can't tell you how often I picked up the phone and put it back down again.

The night I actually did call, I made notes of all the things I wanted to say to her and arranged them around the phone. I must have rehearsed everything a hundred times. This was the toughest performance I had ever prepared for. I was scared of doing something wrong or forgetting something. I was just plain terrified.

She answered the phone. I said quickly, "First thing, I want to give you my name and number," thinking she might hang up on me.

Then I asked her if her birth date was July 12, 1957. She said yes. I asked if the name Constance meant anything to her and she said yes, her birthmother had given her that name but of course it had been changed.

Then she said, "Are you my mother?"

I said, "I believe I am."

It's funny, but I don't even remember what we said next, but we talked that night for an hour, and another hour the next night. We both cried a lot. She started calling me "Mom" right away.

Unfortunately, because I am an expert on the subject, I soon was able to tell that my birthdaughter, whose name is Liz, had been a victim of abuse. She started confiding in me immediately with a trust that usually takes a long time to build.

As it turned out, her brother had sexually abused her for years. This was so ironic and horrible for me. I thought placing her for adoption would guarantee her a better life. She hadn't gone to college either, and that was another thing I had been promised.

Her adoptive mother was very negative about our meeting. She was in the beginning stages of Alzheimer's then, and now remembers nothing, so we'll never know much about her feelings. Her adoptive dad thought it was great that Liz and I had found each other after all these years. He told me little stories about when she was growing up, showed me family photo albums, and always treated me with kindness.

My other children are grown up now and are very accepting of Liz. We all went to the airport to meet her for the first time and my children took turns hugging her. I think they were happy for me and relieved that their mother didn't have to search any more.

My daughter Theresa, soft and tender as ever, said, "It's about time something good like this happened to Mom."

I felt like the circle of my life was made whole again. Every day I still pray in thanksgiving for the incredible gift of my birthdaughter.

Another irony is that my birthdaughter was in the process of a divorce when I met her. Her husband was an alcoholic, and he physically abused her.

They had a thirteen-year-old son, Tad, which made me an instant grandmother. Every possible chance, Liz and Tad came to visit, or we flew to California to visit them. Our relationship became closer and closer.

Liz is the only one of my children who asks my advice—and actually takes it! And of all my children, she is the one who looks most like me. I feel strongly that she has always needed me—and I've always needed her. Now that we're together, we cling to each other like glue.

At her request, I located Rollie, so she could know her birthfather, and have complete answers about nationality and health issues. He and his wife of twenty years were elated to meet Liz. They hadn't been able to have any children together.

I was happy that it worked out so well, and thrilled to learn that Rollie had been dry for ten years. They have formed a special bond and live only two hours apart from each other. Liz thanked me for finding her birthfather and says it makes her feel more complete.

Since Liz and I met, she has remarried and had another son, Teddy. I'm just as crazy about these two boys as I am about my other grandchildren—six in all, plus one great-grandchild!

Because Tad doesn't get along with his stepfather very well, he came to Minneapolis to live with me. We're so proud of him because he's graduated from high school this year. Liz, Teddy, and her husband joined us for a big graduation picnic in Tad's honor. He has a job now, and has a very sweet girlfriend. I would like for him to continue school, but that will have to be Tad's decision. He definitely doesn't want to go back to California, though.

Monica's daughter, my granddaughter, Catherine, and her baby, Sherrie, my great-granddaughter, also live with me, along with my cat and dog. It's a nice big family, much like I used to daydream about when I was little.

I look back at all those years of searching and frustration, and I can't really say it was worth it, because certain things should never happen to anyone. I probably could have benefited from counseling, but I didn't know there was anything different about me. And counseling wasn't very available in those days.

The feeling of abandonment—that everyone would leave me for someone or something else—was constant. Even now, I still have to fight against those feelings.

Every year around Liz's birthday, I used to become physically sick, sometimes bedridden. Since I found her, I am calmer and more at peace. I've even stopped biting my nails. I am thrilled that I have a happy ending to talk about.

Above all, the entire experience of Liz has served to strengthen my faith. Once I gave up the "me" part in my prayers, God seemed to open the door and allow me to find my birthdaughter. I've heard that God makes the cake and lets us add the finishing touches. In my case, I started with a big and confusing bunch of ingredients—but ended up with a wonderfully decorated cake!

Chapter Five

M Y DAD WAS ON A SHIP SOMEWHERE in the North Atlantic when I was born at the Naval Hospital in Norfolk, Virginia, in June of 1943. Since he didn't come home for good until World War II was over, the first three years of my life I was raised by my mom and her parents, who immigrated to the United States from Vienna, Austria. They fled their country just before the war, and since Austria was an Axis country, they had been listed as enemy aliens. I just can't picture that sweet group of people as enemy aliens.

We all lived in Washington, D.C., in my grandparents' home. The family was very European—very close. My mother was the center of my universe. I loved her so much. Maybe too much. I hung on her every word and believed in her completely. Although there was little extra money, we always made a big deal over birthdays, Christmases, and other holidays. Inexpensive or homemade presents were always being passed around.

Mom and my grandparents disciplined verbally and very gently. When I was bad, they would scold me or send me to my room, but they never hit; they didn't believe in physical punishment. They never even raised their voices.

When Dad came home and we moved to Arlington, Virginia, I was terrified of him, especially at first. He believed in spanking, slapping, yelling and screaming when he was angry. After a while it would be over and he'd be fine again. This was quite the contrast to my soft-spoken mother.

I hated my dad's explosive German-Irish temper. But he could also be very loving and affectionate. Dad was always ready with bunches of hugs and kisses for me, and then for my sister Polly, who was born when I was five, and Peter, who came along three years later.

We grew up in a sleepy little neighborhood that was slightly southern, very conservative. In those days, northern Virginia around the Arlington area was mostly homes, shops, churches, schools. Our smallish home always seemed to be overflowing with us kids and our friends. We rode our bikes, played in the woods, built forts and pretended we were soldiers. It was your basic happy childhood—until I started school.

From the time I was very young, I remember people saying I had "two left feet" because I would trip over almost anything, walk into doorframes and walls, and just be generally clumsy. It wasn't until I was in my forties that I was diagnosed as severely learning-disabled. It was found that I had many related problems, including double vision.

Grade school was horrible. I couldn't have possibly understood how I was different from everyone else. School was so much harder for me than it should have been. Unless I really strained, I saw two of everything, side by side. I couldn't sit still. My attention span and recall were nil. I constantly mixed up numbers and couldn't remember directions. If I wasn't physically shown how to do something, I couldn't follow even the simplest of instructions. Everything I was able to learn, I learned by listening and memorizing.

Whenever I was tested, the teachers would say, "The tests show that she's brilliant. She should be an "A" student, rather than just getting by. She must be lazy. She spends too much time daydreaming and too little time paying attention."

Unfortunately, I believed them, which didn't do much for my self-confidence. I was so discouraged. It seemed like the harder I tried, the farther I fell behind, while at the same time my friends went ahead of me by leaps and bounds.

I was lucky I had so many friends. Those friendships brought me a lot of happiness. My best friends were Connie, Dede, Monica, and Marcia. Connie and I were practically inseparable from kindergarten until she moved away when we were about twelve. Dede and Monica were best friends with each other, and Marcia came along for the ride. She ended up being the smartest of us all—taking all the advanced classes and eventually going to Spain as an exchange student. Of all those childhood friendships, Marcia and I are the only ones who have remained close.

Although I hated school because of all the frustrations, I did love music and singing. I found that I was good at acting, most Girl Scout activities, and athletics. And, even though it was hard, I loved learning.

I know now that I must have been a near genius to find all the ways I did to adapt—and actually learn. And it was fortunate that I grew up in an era where reading aloud to the class was a big part of every day. If I could hear it, I could "get" it.

My hopes and dreams for my life were not extravagant. I wanted to get married, raise a family and be a housewife just like my mom. I think I would have been happy doing just that, but things didn't work out quite the way I had imagined.

I guess it's no surprise that I wanted to follow in Mom's footsteps. She was highly organized, softly opinionated and had a tremendous inner strength. I relied on her judgment and was in awe of her abilities. I admired everything about her. She was the very best cook, and I loved to be in the kitchen with her. Mom had tons of patience with my clumsy ways. She allowed me to help cook the meals, cakes, cookies, pies—everything. We were very close. Mom had a way of making everyday life fun.

Our tradition on Christmas Eve was to share a European "cold supper." I loved helping get ready for this day. The house would be cleaned top to bottom. We would set up the Christmas tree and put all the wrapped presents under it. Mom and I made the meal together. All the cold cuts and special Austrian dishes we'd prepared were placed on the table. I always made the chicken livers all by myself because Mom didn't like them.

"Ach!" she'd say. "Don't care for them!"

Mom was wonderful. At supper, in the midst of all our hilarity, she would tell everyone which dishes I had made, saying "Aren't they just the best this year?"

I am so grateful to Mom for giving me confidence in my kitchen abilities. I still feel like there's nothing I can't do in the kitchen.

After supper on Christmas Eve, we'd take hours opening presents, one at a time, making a big production out of each one. Then it was time to clean up and go off to midnight service at church. Christmas Day was spent at Dad's parents' home, with a formal turkey dinner and more presents. Then we all played Michigan Rummy for pennies.

Something else that still brings a smile is our family's camping vacations. What a riot! There was my organized mom, with lists of what everyone was to bring. Each of us was responsible for getting our own things together and packing them into boxes, which we hauled out to the 1955 Chevy station wagon. Then there was my dad, having a cow trying to fit everything in, and us kids making fun of him behind his back without getting caught! Finally, after the car was packed, we were settled in with pillows, books and games, and off we went.

The next scene was "Putting Up the Tent," starring Mr. Temper and Mrs. Cool. Eventually, Dad's sense of humor would overtake his temper and he'd smile at us, and yell, "Charge!"

He would then plunge into the tent with the center pole, and the tent would be up in a flash. That was his signal to go off and fish for the next two weeks. His daily appearances would occur at breakfast, when he presented us with his first catch of the day, and then again at dinner. He always went to bed early and the three of us stayed up playing cards with Mom.

Junior high school was more difficult than grade school. It was transition time, and time to question everything. I'm sorry to admit it, but for the first time I doubted my mother's judgment. Mother—whom I loved and respected above all others!

As I mentioned, Mom was an immigrant, arrived in this country at thirteen and didn't understand this culture. She had no idea how important it was for a girl my age to dress like the other girls. She didn't understand it was crucial to "look right." Instead, she picked out the worst clothes—clunky shoes and garish-colored socks. Because I never had much confidence in my own opinions, I didn't know how to tell her that I hated those clothes, and that they made me look like a square. I mean, couldn't she see that everybody was wearing saddle shoes and bobby socks?

High school was better. I tried out for choir and was accepted. My classes were still very puzzling for me, so most of the time I just got by. I had reached the point where I realized it didn't really matter if I studied or not. I listened as the class discussed each subject, and I remembered only so much. Then I would get confused. Surprisingly, I was able to maintain a "C" average.

One of the great sadness of my life was when my mother's mother died. This was the grandma I had lived with as a baby, and I loved her very much. I was only sixteen and believed that I had somehow caused her death. I had become very ill with mononucleosis and yellow jaundice, and was on complete bed rest. I was sure that I had passed my illness on to her—or because I required so much attention, she didn't get the attention that would have saved her life.

The real story is that tuberculosis had left her with one third of her normal lung function, among other problems. With good medical care, she lived for another twenty years. Then she had to have surgery when her bladder failed. The heart specialist feared that she might not survive the surgery, but she did. Six weeks later, though, she died of heart failure. It was all kind of jumbled, but for a long time afterwards, I blamed myself for her death. I was grief-stricken, and never really got over the loss.

Most families in the 1940s and 1950s did not discuss sex. I knew how cats reproduced, but was never taught about human reproduction or sexuality. At one family event after my sister and I were adults, Mom swore that she had told us everything. At that, Polly and I looked at each other and rolled our eyes, laughing. We had known nothing. And we were afraid to ask. Maybe it was because of my continuing fear of my father's anger, or maybe it was some unspoken taboo or religious thing.

We attended church every Sunday. Apart from family activities, our social events were mainly church-related. I enjoyed all the church things just fine until I discovered boys.

When we were about fourteen, Dede, Monica, Marcia, and I had make-out parties in our basement, the lights low and the music sexy and slow. A lot of boys from school were always eager to attend. The excitement of the forbidden made it all the more enticing for us. Beer was easy to get, we always had a great time and never got caught. We usually went out in groups, breaking into couples to go parking or to drive-in movies. Although we girls really had no idea what we were doing, our social lives revolved around sex.

When we discussed it among ourselves, we agreed that if anyone ever asked us to actually have sex, we would say "no." Because if you did "it" you'd get pregnant.

That time of my life is difficult to explain. Although I did like myself as a person, I felt inferior to all the kids I hung around with, thinking they were so much smarter than me. I carried around the guilt of my grandmother's death, and missed her terribly. Somehow, I decided that sex would help me feel better. I was sixteen. I convinced myself that I needed to do "it." I looked over my circle of boyfriends and picked out a likely candidate. The rest was easy, and I was lucky enough to not get pregnant.

During my senior year of high school, I took a night class at a local university. There was a young man in my class who was very attractive to me. His name was Anthony and he was a full-time student, majoring in sociology. Anthony assumed that I was a college student, too, and I never told him I was still in high school. We went to his apartment two or three times a week and had great sex. Anthony would then take me home in his white Jaguar XKE. He was as cool as his car, and I was crazy about him.

On graduation night, Chuck, a boy I knew from my homeroom class, asked me to go out with him after graduation exercises. I jumped at the chance, having always thought of Chuck as drop-dead good looking. We went parking in his car, drank way too much beer and ended up having sex.

The next morning was filled with activity, because our family was moving to a new house. It was a bigger, much nicer home, and I looked forward to all sorts of happy times in it.

I hadn't been paying any attention to the regularity of my periods. After all, I had been sexually active for a long time, and I hadn't gotten pregnant, so I wasn't worried. But by the end of July, I knew I was pregnant.

I called Anthony to tell him, and his answer was, "It couldn't be me. I've been sterile since a diving accident in Hawaii. Have you been with anyone else?"

I panicked and hung up. Now that I look back on it, I was foolish to have believed him. I still don't know if he told me the truth or not. People were always taking advantage of me like that.

The rest of the summer passed in a sick daze. I was having morning sickness and sometimes evening sickness, too. I hibernated in the "rec room" of our nice new house. I did nothing and told no one about my problem. Since I wasn't showing yet, I even started college in the fall, living at home and pretending nothing was wrong.

When Mom confronted me in October, my pregnancy was pretty hard to deny. I was about five months along, and starting to pop out. My parents were very upset. They both cried. Mom said that she wished I had told her sooner, so that she could try to arrange an abortion through her contacts in Europe. Abortion was still illegal here in this country.

"Or," Mom said, "I could have pretended to be pregnant myself, so we could keep the baby."

I'm not sure that I could have lived with either of those options. I believed Anthony about not being the father, and I certainly didn't want to marry Chuck, who had gotten me drunk and used me.

I was afraid to tell my parents that Chuck was the father, in case they tried to force me to marry him. They kept after me, though, and eventually, I gave in and told them about Chuck and how it happened. My father called Chuck's father and told him that he'd take care of everything—but that Chuck's father should know what his son had done.

Mom and Dad took me to our pastor's office. I felt like I was invisible. My parents and the pastor made the decision that my baby would be adopted. The pastor suggested a specific adoption agency and my parents knew people who had adopted through this agency. They knew that this particular agency did a thorough investigation of prospective parents. They wanted my baby to be raised in our Lutheran religion by loving parents.

The next thing that happened was that I was sent to a home for unwed mothers in a town near Arlington. When I first got there, I was in some kind of shock or complete denial. I barely looked pregnant, I didn't feel pregnant, and I certainly didn't want to be pregnant at eighteen! But there I was, with about twenty-five other girls who were in the same boat.

At first I didn't bathe very often, because my towels kept disappearing. Everything was pretty grim until Lynn arrived. She took me under her wing and taught me how to fend for myself. She also taught me how to do laundry and how to protect my towels. I guess it was pretty obvious that I'd never been away from home. Then, when Karen arrived, Lynn and I took charge of her. She was in worse shape emotionally than I had been. The three of us became very close. Lynn and I remained friends for years. She was one of the best friends I've ever had.

There were strict rules at The Home. We had to sign in and out, and were required to eat all our meals together. We weren't supposed to exchange names and addresses, but Lynn, Karen and I did. It was a strange way to live. We were all just waiting to give birth and then leave.

Lynn had a girl and decided to keep her baby. I felt so lonely after she left. One day, a social worker came to visit. She did some psychological tests on me, but she didn't counsel me, give me any alternatives to adoption or encourage me to keep my baby.

I was trying to be a good girl, to get back into everyone's good graces, and I felt like this was God's punishment for having sex—having to give my baby up. My pastor and my mother told me that adoption was the right thing to do. And I really didn't even know how to question my mother's judgment.

Despite the trauma, I look back on that time as one of the happiest of my whole life. I loved being pregnant. I enjoyed it. The only way I can explain it is that I felt at peace with the world.

Back home, my predicament was a Big Secret. My sister and brother had no idea what was going on and none of my friends knew. My parents and Dad's parents came to visit occasionally, and Mom called me on the phone every day. My dear grandfather took me out to dinner every Sunday, but he never said much.

The doctors thought my due date was in February, but February came and went—no baby. Of course, who knew exactly when I had become pregnant? My labor pains finally started on the afternoon of March 3, 1962. I was sent to the hospital alone. I remember watching a doctor show on TV during the first part of my labor, which wasn't very painful at all, and thinking "Hey, this isn't so bad!"

It was decided that I wasn't progressing quickly enough, so my labor was induced. I was taken to the delivery room and heavily sedated. I don't remember a thing, but was told that my daughter was born at 12:10 a.m. on March 4.

When I woke up, I felt like I had been cut in half. It was so awful. But then the nurses started bringing my baby in for all the regular feedings, and I forgot all about the pain. What a quiet and beautiful baby she was! For the next few days I held her and fed her. It was wonderful. I even had my mother crochet a little outfit for her.

I lied to my hospital roommate about my situation, pretending I was a happily married young woman whose husband was, unfortunately, out of town when I went into labor. I didn't want her to think I was a slut.

On the fourth day after my baby's birth, a social worker came bearing papers. I filled in the birth certificate with my name, my baby's name and Chuck as father. I named my daughter Beryl Anne, not because I particularly liked the name, but because I knew someone named Beryl at The Home. I didn't want to choose a name that would be too close to my heart. I signed the temporary placement papers, dressed my daughter and we left the hospital—in different directions.

I returned to The Home to recover for a couple of weeks. The social worker came to visit me again and I signed the final papers. She shook my hand and wished me well. Following through with my mother's plan, I flew to Connecticut to visit the aunt I was supposed to have been staying with for those months. The story was that I was helping her take care of her new baby. I stayed with my aunt for about two weeks before returning home to my parents' house.

Everybody was so happy to have me back home again. My parents never spoke about the baby or the adoption. I built a sort of cement wall inside myself to hide my feelings. I went into some kind of funk. I didn't know then what was going on, but it was like I wasn't quite all there—like a piece was missing. There was a terrible guilt—like I had become a second-class person unworthy of a good life. I have some knowledge now about what was happening to me, but I wish I had understood more then. It would have given me more control over what was to come.

After my "unfortunate break," as my parents referred to it, they decided to send me to secretarial school. I was still in a fog, probably clinically depressed. I went along with what they wanted, sort of dated, but just floated along, with not much interest in anything or anyone. I muddled through school for a year. Then, at twenty, I started working for the government.

I began as a "GS-3" at the Department of the Interior and got an apartment with another girl. I had a terrible time being a secretary, but it wasn't for lack of trying. Anyone with a learning disability would recognize my problems, but I didn't know I had learning disabilities—or even what that was. My attention span was still bad, I had a hard time sitting still, and I couldn't remember the order in which to do things. I was great at dealing with complex problems, but I really messed up the simple tasks. Amazingly, I held that job for thirteen years.

In keeping with my "second-class" mentality, I settled for far less than the best. I picked the wrong friends, the wrong boyfriends, the wrong job . . . I even married the wrong man.

Through a mutual friend, I met Mark at a party. I could tell that he liked me right away, but he said we had to wait, because he was entangled in a "marriage of convenience" to a very young girl who lived with his two-year-old baby in California.

We began dating anyway, and I was so impressed that someone actually wanted me, that I never made a decision about what I wanted. Mark moved in with me after a few months. Our first big fight ended with me apologizing. This was the start of something really bad. I apologized for everything, always trying to make things right. I should have stuck up for myself, but I just took all his guilty baggage along with my own, and when things got worse, I just worked harder to make it okay. But it was never okay.

Mark and I were married in April 1968 at Our Redeemer Lutheran Church—my church—in Falls Church, Virginia. I was twenty-four. We had a beautiful wedding and a boring honeymoon in St. Thomas. There wasn't anything to do, and we didn't enjoy each other's company all that much.

Mark was very moody—running either hot or cold. I never knew what to expect. I tried to create a normal life for myself and went through the motions. On Wednesday evenings was choir practice, Saturday mornings laundry, and I got my hair done on Saturday afternoons. I handled the lawn and the garden, we shared the cooking and cleaning. I thought our life together, though dull, was tolerable. Our sex life was less than perfect. He never took time for my needs. Behind his back, I used to refer to him as "the rabbit." I really loved him, though.

Mark was upset about my never becoming pregnant. I did become pregnant once, though. Mark didn't believe me at first, but I knew right away there was something wrong. The doctor put me on complete bed rest with pills for the pain and pills to help me sleep, but I lost the baby anyway. In fact, I almost died as well. It was an ectopic (tubal) pregnancy.

Apparently, Mark felt sorry enough for himself during that time to justify his having an affair. My parents couldn't even find him when they took me to the hospital. While I was fighting for my life, he was having sex with some other woman.

When I finally went home, I had lost forty pounds in three months and was terribly weak. Then the phone calls began. It was "her," and she'd hang up if I answered. I knew I should leave Mark, but no one in my family had ever been divorced. I convinced myself that if I could just bear with it, things would somehow get better.

One time, I even became forceful with him, delivering the ultimatum, "her or me." But we just went on as usual. I never got pregnant again. I thought about adoption. I had this feeling that since I had given up a child to adoption, I deserved another from someone else. With the two-year wait, and the way things were, I never pursued it aggressively.

Without consulting me, Mark applied for a job with the Baltimore Colts football team, which would involve moving and me having to change jobs. He was offered the job and accepted it before even notifying me. I found us a house in Baltimore and a moving company. My parents helped me get everything ready, and all of our possessions were moved in before Mark even saw the house.

I got a job as a secretary for Social Security. Mark continued to have affairs behind my back. I threatened to leave him for good if he didn't stop. Our relationship became more and more distant. It seemed to me that he had a confused view of reality, which was becoming a problem. He lost his job with the Colts, and then went on to a series of jobs, none of which he could hold for more than six months.

I started getting headaches from the pressure of working sixty to seventy hours a week in order to make our financial obligations. Mark's typical day was watching television, taking care of the dog and puppies, smoking and drinking beer.

His drinking was becoming a problem, but he said, "If it bothers you, then it's your problem."

Mark badgered me and demeaned me in front of everyone. He made fun of me all the time. I found evidence of still another girlfriend, which he tried to deny. At that point, there seemed so little left of our marriage, that I called the movers and my parents and had them pack me up and take me back home. Mark and I were married for nine years at the time of our divorce.

I moved back to Virginia and in with my parents. In spite of everything, I still loved Mark tremendously. But I knew he was going downhill, and I didn't want to go with him. He loved me, too, and told me so years later after he had remarried. Our relationship couldn't last because it was just too destructive.

I got my own apartment again. I began to travel, took scuba lessons and went on diving trips. I did almost anything to try to escape from my real world. I tried drugs and drinking, but they didn't fill the void. I was real good at sex, but not good at intimacy.

I had built a wall around myself and nobody was going to get in. I kept everyone at arm's length, including my family. I was not happy with this sort of life. I was just existing day to day.

I finally found out about my learning disabilities when I was in my mid-forties. Polly's son, my nephew, was being tested, and they said it ran in families—had anyone else been diagnosed? Neither my sister nor my brother-in-law had any symptoms. My sister shared all this information with me, which started me thinking.

I had just barely survived a performance review at work, with a less than outstanding rating because I "constantly mixed up phone numbers, forgot half the instructions given and forgot assignments." I was in tears. I called a school for people with learning disabilities, and made an appointment to be tested. I figured it couldn't hurt.

At the appointment, I was diagnosed immediately with several learning disabilities. I remember sitting there and crying with relief. It was like a light suddenly went on in my life.

The director patiently explained what each disability meant in regards to how my world works. He explained that "LD" people don't learn or even think like other people do. He said that the tests also showed me to be near genius. He was amazed at the degree to which I had taught myself to learn. He said most people with such severe disabilities don't even make it through junior high school!

I was referred to a special eye doctor, who couldn't believe I worked with computers and graphics for a living. According to her tests, I don't see things like other people do. I'll never forget her words, "You must be made of piss and vinegar to have accomplished so much!"

It was the first time my accomplishments had ever been recognized, except by my mother. The doctor prescribed special glasses. I was astonished at the difference they made. No more headaches, no more awful eye strain.

Now a lot of things about my life made sense, including my insecurity and my inability to make decisions. I knew why everything had always been so hard for me.

I attended adult classes at the school for about two years. I tested at the college level in reading comprehension and math. My poor ego was certainly boosted by that.

A few years before my big discovery, I started attending a search/support group for women who had lost a child through adoption. I had visited the adoption agency, and they had provided all the standard non-identifying information. In fact, the social worker had left me alone in the room with the file folder. Being as naive as I was, it never occurred to me to "peek."

I didn't actively search for my daughter at first because of the walls I'd so painfully built, and because I didn't think I deserved the happiness of finding her. But after I found out about my learning disabilities, I knew that I needed to find her, because of the possibility of her having inherited the LD monster. The growth and wisdom I was beginning to find helped me give myself permission to complete my search.

Since the adoption took place in Washington, D.C., where all the records are sealed, I found an underground "searcher" through another birthmother.

One day when my parents were outside gardening, I approached them about my decision to search for my daughter.

"That's nice," my mother said, without looking up.

"What? What?" said my dad, who is hard of hearing.

"She wants to find her daughter. You know, the adopted one."

Then they told me if I needed any money, nothing was too much. I should just let them know. They said that my daughter and I needed to find each other.

It was expensive. My parents just handed me the money—no questions asked. Within a day or two of my forwarding the money, the searcher called me to verify the information I already had. Two days later I got another call with complete information on my daughter. Her name was Linnea and she lived in Kansas.

It was the beginning of a whole new life for me. It was, in a way, the beginning of my life. I was forty-seven. Linnea was twenty-nine. I called her for the first time on a January night of 1992. I had a pad of paper nearby so I could take notes.

"Is this Linnea Martinson?"

"Yes. Who is this?"

"My name is Arlene Griggs. Were you born on March 4th, 1962?"

"Yes."

"I had a baby on that day and placed her for adoption. I believe that you might be that baby."

She was crying. I was crying. I heard her husband in the background asking what was wrong.

"It's my mother," she replied. "My real mother."

I'll never forget how I felt to hear those words. Her existence was a reality! We talked for a long time. I found out that she had recently started searching for me. We made plans to talk again the next day, after she had time to digest everything.

It was like a honeymoon, only not at all boring this time. We exchanged letters, phone calls, photographs . . . she is so beautiful. I found out that I was a grandmother, too. We made plans for me to fly out to Kansas the following month, and to share Linnea's thirtieth birthday with her and her family.

Linnea met me at the airport with an armful of flowers. There I was, forty-five pounds overweight, feeling ugly and worrying about what she'd think of me—and all she could do was grin! We had a great visit. I got to rock my sweet baby grandson to sleep.

Linnea's adoptive mother was very supportive at first about us being reunited. Linnea's sister Diane, who was also adopted, was in the process of looking for her biological roots, too.

There were no other children in the family. The adoptive mother had been a medical technician, the father a high school teacher. At the time they adopted Linnea, they lived in northern Virginia—about a quarter of a mile from my parents' home. The father taught in the high school my sister attended. So much coincidence.

When Linnea was about four, her adoptive father had returned to school and became a Lutheran minister. Until his health failed, the family had moved from state to state to serve various congregations. A heavy smoker, her father developed heart trouble, and died when Linnea was a senior in high school.

I flew Linnea and the baby back to Virginia for my parents' fiftieth wedding anniversary party. It was a boisterous, happy house—full of friends and relatives—which smoothed over the announcement of "Oh, by the way, Arlene had a baby, placed her for adoption and here she is."

Virtually no one had known about Linnea, but everyone seemed happy. My sister took my hand and said, "Now this is the Arlene I used to know. There's a joy about you now—no more sadness."

I've been smiling ever since I found my daughter. She is a lot like me—intellectually inquiring and physically active. She loved it when they lived in Oklahoma, where she was a cheerleader for her high school wrestling team. Before moving to Kansas, she attended college in Oklahoma and met her future husband there.

Linnea's mother seemed very interested in all the similarities of our families at first, but after we met, her interest seemed to cool. Some time in 1994, my relationship with my daughter started to change. After being so close and involved in each other's lives, Linnea informed me that her mother was very insecure about our relationship.

"She's uneasy about 'us' and doesn't want to hear about 'us' any more," Linnea said, hesitantly.

I know she didn't want to hurt my feelings. After that our phone conversations became labored as she became more and more distant. I wrote to my daughter, letting her know that I didn't like things this way, but that I would accept anything she felt she needed to do. I did not receive a reply.

Mom said I'd hear from her again after her adoptive mother dies. I really didn't like the idea of waiting around for someone to die, but there's nothing I could do about the situation. At Christmas, I send a family-type gift to Linnea, her husband, and my grandson. Every March, I send a huge bouquet of flowers with a card that reads, "Happy Birthday. Love, Arlene."

I have a good career as secretary to three officers at the Federal Reserve Board. My work with graphics remains fascinating to me. I test new software programs and teach classes about how to use them. Imagine—me—the learning disabled one, teaching others!

No matter what happens, my entire life has changed because of finding my daughter. I am a whole person again. To this day, though, I cannot believe that I allowed my parents and pastor to take my child away. I can't alter what was, and I have very little control over the future, but at least I am no longer in the dark. I feel good about myself now, and am no longer ashamed of having had a baby. I have lost weight, and I look forward to the future for the first time. I am making real plans about the rest of my life, rather going through the fog, day by day.

My sister Polly and I are very close now. I may even retire in California where she is living so we can be together. As for my folks, Dad has become very religious and thoughtful of others. He remembers all the details Mom now forgets. They are a perfect team, and their roles have adjusted with age. Dad is the one who keeps in contact with everybody—calling or writing if he hasn't heard from us in a while.

I love music, theater, movies, and my dog, Bruno. I even love to read, although I'm very slow at it. My activities are a little less combative than they used to be, but I still dive, ride bike and do some aerobics and weight training. I enjoy potting, when I have access to a wheel and kiln. And I'm still my mother's daughter—I still love to cook. I have assisted chefs at a professional cooking school, and may go to chef's school when I retire.

I don't have the relationship with my daughter that I want to have—that I did have for almost two years. But I still feel that we are connected. I feel it in my soul that we will be reunited some day.

This all has been unbelievably painful for me to remember and go over again. My fondest wish is that Linnea will soon open the door again and say, "Come on in."

But for now, I have found her, and that needs to be enough.

Chapter Six

JUDITH

I DIDN'T KNOW UNTIL I WAS A TEENAGER that my dad had been "dropped off." That's how he put it. Nobody ever talked about it.

When my mom let me in on the family's deep, dark secret, she instructed me, "Never mention this to your father."

And I didn't. Not for years and years.

Dad was born in 1922 in Spartanburg, South Carolina, to a dentist who had been very recently married to a fine woman of "good standing." My father was born one month early—a little too soon after the wedding. His birthparents thought it best for everyone concerned that he be given up for others to raise. The baby was brought to a hospital in Ashville, North Carolina, where Nurse Emma worked. He weighed only four pounds. Nurse Emma watched over her new charge and, when he didn't seem to thrive, she asked for breast milk donations from all the nursing mothers in the hospital. Baby Brooks survived, and Emma became very attached to him.

When she decided it was time for her to move back to her home state of Minnesota, Emma received permission from Brooks' birthfather to take the baby home and continue caring for him. As a professional woman—and single, Emma didn't feel that she alone could give Brooks all the care he deserved. She asked her sister and brother-in-law to take him in. They raised him through high school, with financial support from Emma, and then from Emma and "Doc" when Emma eventually married. There was never a formal adoption at the time because Emma couldn't convince the dentist to sign the necessary papers. There were a few letters exchanged. This is part of one, dated March 6, 1923:

I received your letter today and was mighty glad to hear from you and to know that the baby is doing fine. The reason I have not returned the papers is that I just haven't been able to bring up the subject to my wife and also because we cannot get anyone to sign these here since I want the matter kept a secret—it would just ruin us for it to be known. I have been thinking of going to Atlanta and get these fixed up there but have not been able to get away . . . We have been trying to forget and we never mention the subject to each other . . . I wish there were some way for me to get out of asking my wife to sign the papers, couldn't some way be arranged? We would never try to claim the child, I can promise you that. I just hate to ask my wife, we are beginning to be happy again . . . I want to thank you and express my appreciation for your kindness . . .

How sad that they couldn't even talk about it together, and that it would ruin them in their community if anyone knew about the baby. Continuing the lies and cover up, the truth about my dad's background was never discussed in the family. The fact that he had been "dropped off" was always a source of shame for him.

Brooks used Emma's sister's last name while growing up. Emma and Doc continued to support him and be his parents. When World War II broke out, my father wanted to enlist in the army. It took some time and effort but Doc and Emma helped him to secure his original birth certificate, which the army required, and that is when he assumed his original surname.

Doc was a medical doctor without, it had been said, much of a bedside manner, so he switched to real estate after the war. He did well in his new career. Since housing was in short supply at that time, Doc bought old mansions in Owatonna, Rochester, and Waseca and had them converted into apartment buildings. He built a four-plex in St. Paul called Montrose Place, and that was where he and Emma lived.

My father decided to get into real estate, too. He married my mom in 1946, when they were both twenty-four. Brooks and Joan had a beautiful love story. She was a sweet Southern girl, and he was tall and handsome, with striking blue eyes and black hair.

I was born about a year after their wedding day. An only child, I spent a lot of time playing alone—coloring, mostly. I always loved art and the idea of creating things with my imagination. My other favorite thing to do was go visit Grandma Emma and Doc. Emma was a natural caregiver and everyone loved her. I see her as Kuan Yin, the goddess of compassion. Like Kuan Yin, Emma held all the cares of the world in a vessel cupped in her hands. As you'll find out later in my story, our close relationship lasted long after she left this world—until the present day, in fact.

Emma and I played games that she invented for my enjoyment. She'd turn me loose in the kitchen, give me an assortment of strange ingredients like corn starch, sugar, and salt, and then encourage me to mix up a "mystery meal," which Doc, joining in the game, would pretend to eat. She'd take the crystals off the chandelier and let me play with them. I listened to everyone's heartbeat with Doc's old stethoscope and sorted old pills according to

size, color, and shape. I had the run of the house and was well loved and cared for. Emma's nephew, Brookie, who was named after my father, often joined us in play. Two years older than me, Brookie was like my brother. Unfortunately, he fought depression all his life and committed suicide at age thirty-two. I still miss him.

Although I loved my art classes, I was eager to finish school. I liked what I liked and what I didn't like I was bored with. I hated the controlling factor of school. I wanted to get out into the real world. I couldn't wait to be on my own.

Wanting to be out in the real world.

At age seventeen I graduated from high school and moved away from home. It wasn't very far away, though—the efficiency apartment right next door to my parents' apartment. But anyway, I was on my own! I had some odd jobs, was a model for an art school and worked at Brown & Bigelow in the photography department.

My parents allowed me the illusion of being on my own until one Saturday night when I didn't come home. I had become a "theater rat," involved in whatever I could do to be part of the local theater scene. On that particular Saturday night, I was playing a Jewish beatnik in *Take Her, She's Mine.* After the performance there was a cast party, which ended up lasting all night. I came home the next day, purely innocent, to Mom and Dad's wrath. They had been terribly worried. At first I didn't understand, but that day I learned a valuable lesson about being sensitive to people's feelings.

I continued having fun with my theater colleagues, including my dear friend, Bob. One night after another party, Bob and I caught a ride with a guy who, as it turned out, was probably too drunk to drive. By the time we got to my house, Bob was talking about taking the bus home.

"Do you want to stay here?" I asked, not even thinking we'd sleep together.

"Okay. I'll stay," said Bob.

One thing led to another, I guess. And that was that. But then, I didn't get my period. What's going on? And then I didn't get it again! I thought, I'll get it next time. This cannot be happening. People don't get pregnant when they have sex only once and for the first time. Seriously, I thought I'd wake up one morning and it would all be a dream. There goes my colorful imagination again. To complicate things further, my wonderful Emma had just died, from complications of a stroke. I was lost and in denial.

I had known a couple of girls who'd had abortions. I even knew where to find the woman who performed the abortions. One day I got her phone number. I picked up the phone, dialed her number and hung up. I couldn't do it. I hid my condition well with oversized shirts, but I knew I couldn't hide it forever.

Bob and I went to a play with another couple. We went to Embers afterwards for a snack. When I dropped my napkin on the floor, and Bob and I leaned over at the same time to pick it up, I whispered to him, "You're going to be a father."

We continued the conversation with our friends, and talked about it later when we were alone.

"I'm not too surprised," said Bob. "I knew something was going on."

Bob thought I should see a doctor, and he got me the name of one he thought I could trust. I made an appointment and told the doctor my story. He was kind and understanding. I developed a big crush on him.

My doctor strongly suggested that I tell my parents. I knew he was right, so I wrote them a letter and slipped it under their apartment door. It was a long letter, explaining everything and ending with, "Everybody is healthy, Bob is the father, I'll go away if you want, or I'll stay, and that Bob and I have decided together to place the baby for adoption."

I went back to my apartment and waited.

Mom came over first. She was shocked and disappointed.

"How could you ever do that?" she asked. "Dad will be over as soon as he gets home from work."

I waited some more.

Dad was gentle. "It sounds like you've gotten yourself into a little bit of trouble." Then he took my hand.

My parents decided that I should stay in my apartment and keep the whole thing secret. They owned the apartment building so it would be necessary for me to hide from the tenants. They contacted the Welfare Department for adoption information and were referred to the Children's Home Society of Minnesota. The Children's Home Society (CHS) arranged for me to see a counselor. Every two weeks I went to see Mr. Fred, a psychologist. He explained the adoption process to me, answered all my questions and tried to match my wishes to an appropriate family. I was very comfortable with our adoption decision.

Doc thought I was "cold" to give up my baby. "Emma would not approve of you doing this," he said, more than once.

A lot of guilt was being ladled out, but I never felt guilty, thanks to the support I had, and to all the counseling.

On January 22, 1967, I woke up early and told my mom, "This is it." I called Bob to tell him I was going to the hospital. I wore a fake wedding ring and the hospital put a wristband on me that said "Mrs." I was in labor for six hours or so.

Birthing was definitely not for me.

When Bob arrived he said, "You look terrible."

I said, "I'm going to adopt all my children from now on." But I never had any other children. This was my one and only.

Mom and Bob saw the baby but I didn't. Mr. Fred had advised against it. The doctor had told me that it was a very healthy baby boy with ten fingers and ten toes. When I went home several days later, there was a huge ice storm with thunder and lightning. The next day the trees were coated with ice that glimmered in the sunshine. I felt fantastic. So relieved that the baby was healthy. A family had been notified and would get him within two weeks. I was very comfortable with that and so was Bob.

Mr. Fred gave me a photo of the baby taken on the day he left the hospital. I looked at that photo a lot. My one regret is that I didn't name him because "Baby Boy" on the birth certificate sounds so uncaring. I would have named him Brooks. His adoptive parents, Claudia and Loyal, named him Brent. That's pretty close.

I decided on art school. Doc said he'd pay for my education. I had known since I was little that a career in the art world was for me. I knew I wanted to make a living with my artwork, which led me into my career as an art director and designer. It's still exciting to me—to be able to make a living just "coloring." I started off working for some advertising agencies and, after some years, started my own design business.

I moved into Emma and Doc's old building, Montrose Place, after they had both passed on. I could feel their spirits in that apartment. I had inherited some of their furniture, including two lamps—one candelabra style and one hand-carved wooden spiral, which Emma had rewired. Often at night, those two lamps would flicker, and I knew Emma was there, playing with the lights. Before I moved into my house in 1979, I sat down in Emma's rocking chair and remembered something Emma had told me a long time ago.

"When I die," she had said, "I'm going to come back and haunt you. In a good way."

I knew that she never wanted to lose me. Right there in Emma's rocker, I invited them both to move in with me, and they did. Emma and Doc are always good company. In the new house, those lamps continued to flicker, even after I had them rewired. There goes Emma, playing with the lights again.

In 1986 I was thirty-nine and my son was nineteen. For several years I had been looking at boys his age and wondering, is that him? That could be him. He might be tall like that boy. He might look like me.

Finally, I called Children's Home Society and told them that I would be open to a meeting with him, if that's what he might want. The following week, I found a message on my phone.

"This is CHS," said the voice on the machine. "Call me back."

What's CHS? I wondered. A solicitation? It finally dawned on me that it was Children's Home Society.

I called them back. It seems that my son's file had been recently opened because he had called about me the previous month. I was overwhelmed about how tuned in we were to each other. After being apart for all these years.

I met with Meg Bale, a CHS "post-adoption" counselor. She explained to me about the change in Minnesota adoption law and the process that CHS used. I was instructed that my son and I should exchange photos and letters first, going through the office, and then arrange a time to meet in person.

After a great deal of thought, I composed a letter. I wrote it from my heart but tried to keep it light, with a bit of humor. His letter was very sweet. He said he always knew he would meet me some day. He talked about his girlfriend, Heidi, how she was the best thing that had ever happened to him and how anxious he was for me to meet her. We both wanted our face-to-face meeting to happen soon.

My father was against the idea of my meeting my son. His birth-parents had never contacted him—a clean break. "You don't know what you're getting into," Dad cautioned. "Don't do it."

Mom, on the other hand, was all for it. I had talked with her about it over the years and we both believed that it was inevitable that my son and I meet.

It was in a little meeting room at CHS. It was going to be just the two of us. Meg had advised me that his mother was very involved and I should be ready for that. I was shown into the room, given some coffee, was told to relax and that he'd be there shortly.

There was a quiet knock on the door. There was my baby—six-foot-two, wearing cowboy boots that added a couple more inches to his height. I couldn't take my eyes off him.

"Let's just sit and look at each other for a little," I said.

After that, we shared family photos and talked and talked.

Then he said, "Let's get out of here. My mom wants to meet you."

The three of us went to lunch at the Malt Shop, where we ate and talked for hours. We made a plan to meet again the next day. On that day we sat on my deck and talked about everything. Brent had a lot of questions. I hadn't told Bob yet about the meeting because I wanted to make sure things would be comfortable. I quickly realized that everything was going to be fine.

Claudia was pregnant with Brent's sister Stacy when he was adopted, so they are almost the same age. His brother Ross was a few years older and younger sister Heather was born with developmental disabilities. I so admire Claudia's strength. She supported her husband, Loyal, through cancer treatment while raising Ross, Brent, Stacy, and Heather. Loyal died when Brent was thirteen.

Claudia asked me when my birthday was and I responded, "July 11."

"What?" she exclaimed. "That's my birthday, too!"

I love Claudia and consider her my soul sister.

When Brent met my dad for the first time, Dad was very uncomfortable, but after a while, he was getting used to the idea. He started to believe things would work out, and that's when he began facing his own

Buddies.

background for the first time. He started talking more openly about his past and even told Brent about his being "dropped off."

We began inviting Brent and his adoptive family to our lake cabin near Brainerd. My dad had undergone surgery to repair a hole in his heart, and that hole was healing, both literally and figuratively. At the cabin, Dad taught Brent, who looks remarkably like him, how to take care of everything there—the dock, the plumbing and general maintenance. They became buddies.

We all attended Brent and Heidi's wedding and have shared every birthday, special event and holiday with Brent, Claudia, and the family ever since. After a whole lifetime of being an only child, I now had a son, a daughter-in-law, a soul sister and the rest of the wonderful extended family. We have really become one family.

In 1995, Anika, my first granddaughter was born. In 1999, Brent and Heidi became parents of premature twin girls. Madison and Ellie

A close-knit and loving family, after all these years.

shared my mother's birth date. To everyone's great sadness, Ellie didn't live. There was a funeral with a tiny white casket. In 2001, Isaac was born to this happy and grateful family. To our three precious grandchildren, we are and have always been "Grandma Judith and Grandpa Bob."

Brent is a photographer and director of Creative Services—an artist like me. Heidi is an elementary school teacher. The children are all sensitive, artistic and beautiful, of course. They live in a small town in southern Minnesota, close enough for us to see each other regularly.

We've all lived through so much over the years. My dad's stroke, which led to early onset Alzheimer's, the loss of little Ellie, my mom's health issues and in 2011, the death of the very precious person, Brent's sister Heather.

In January 1999, my dad's condition had become terminal. The hospice team told us that the time was near. Dad wasn't able to communicate at all. He was using all his energy to stay alive. Brent, Heidi, Anika, Mom, a few friends, and I had been with Dad at the nursing home all day. It had been a long day. As we all made our way to the door, Brent hesitated and said he wanted to go back to see Dad, his buddy, one more time.

During those last few minutes Brent took Dad's hand and told him not to worry about anything, promising he would take care of everybody. Brent said Dad looked straight into his eyes and winked, letting Brent know that he understood.

We all left after that. I dropped Mom off and went home. About a half hour later I received a call from the nursing home. They said that Dad had finally been able to let go, and had passed away.

Brent has always kept his promise.

Chapter Seven

SHIRLEY

MY SISTER, MUFF, AND I GREW UP in what we grimly called, "The Sanitorium." It was rather a dreary existence for both of us, and an unusual way for children to be raised, to put it mildly.

I was born in Boston in 1929, six months before my father was diagnosed with tuberculosis. By the time I was four, it became clear that he would never recover, and my mother thought it best to move to Pennsylvania where his family lived.

Our new ten-room house was big and airy, with a giant elm tree in the front. This old elm was the largest tree in the area, and it became very special to me. For years, when I was upset about things, I would sit at its base and just let my thoughts go. My tree was also the first in the area to contract the dreaded Dutch Elm disease. I was so upset when they cut it down.

Mother began transforming the rooms, one by one, into sickrooms as terminally ill relatives started moving in with us. Arthritic and elderly Great Aunt Maggie was first and of course, there was my father. As his disease worsened, he was admitted to hospitals and sent home over and over again. Poor Father. I never knew him as a father—only an invalid. He and I really had no relationship at all. I was only twelve when he died. My sister, Marilyn, whom we all called "Muff," was six when he died, so neither of us ever really had a father.

After Father died, it was somehow determined that Mother was the only one in our extended family who was able-bodied enough to handle sick people. And heaven knows, we had the space. Society was different in the 1930s and 1940s. Family members relied more on each other than they do now. When people had trouble, they went to their families expecting to be taken in.

Next to arrive were the grandparents. Grandmother and Grandfather Munson came as a set. I believe they had heart trouble, as did Grandmother and Grandfather Holbrook, whose stays overlapped with the other grandparents'. My mother's sisters, Aunt Liza and Aunt Lorraine both had cancer, as I recall. Father's brother Daniel and his wife, Elaine, had severe health problems due to excessive drinking. With the exception of Aunt Maggie, who spent the last few weeks of her life in a nursing home, all of these people died in our house.

The atmosphere was often hushed and gloomy. I can still hear my mother's voice reminding us "Never talk in a loud voice" and "Don't run in the house" and "Don't walk with a heavy step." Mother was a good soul, and we were quite close. She always tried to make time for me between Aunt Maggie's feedings and Aunt Lorraine's sponge bath—or whenever she could spare a few minutes. Sometimes I'd follow her around and we'd chat while she changed bedclothes, refilled water bottles and performed other seemingly endless chores.

Muff and I were not particularly close, partly because of the age difference. We were also treated very differently. With her delicate bone structure and soft blonde curls, Muff was the protected, dainty daughter. There were always grandparents, aunts, and uncles, all in various stages of decay and decline, who had the time and inclination to teach "Little Muffie" the refined niceties of life. Muff learned cooking, sewing, needlework, piano, and fine manners.

As the older child in a fatherless family I was treated as the man of the family and was expected to handle the heavy work around the house. I was groundskeeper and handyman, always working alone, my mind stagnant from lack of contact with other people. At the tender age of nine, I was already changing storms and screens, hauling them to and from the garage, up the rungs of the ladder and hanging them in the appropriate windows. I also mowed the lawn and painted the house—indoors and out.

Consequently, I became a tomboy, and though I was mostly a solemn and solitary child, I did have a few boys as pals.

There were several unspoken rules in our household. We were never to argue with anyone or criticize anyone or anything. Nor were we to show any emotion whatsoever. It was a Puritanical environment. Conversations or even idle comments regarding dressing, undressing, getting ready for bed, or any act performed in the bathroom were all strictly forbidden. We were not allowed to talk about the body at all, so of course talking about sex was taboo.

Since I was taught nothing about my body and nothing about sexuality, I was left to conjure up my own images and beliefs. I'm not sure where my ideas came from, but I believed that people's sexuality existed only in the sanctity of the marital bed. I believed that only in the union of marriage could a child be conceived. Of course it would be a sin to enjoy sex except in the sacrosanct domain of husband and wife.

I had little or no social life in grade school. I wasn't allowed to invite my few friends to my house, and I wouldn't have wanted to. Nobody would have had very much fun in that funereal environment. I pretended that I lived in a normal household, and made up excuses if anyone wanted to come over. In those days it was not appropriate for a girl to be as masculine as the role I was forced to play, so I hid that part of my life, too. I developed strong coping skills, which helped me—for a time.

My teachers were impressed with how quickly I learned. I was always at the top of my class, and even was able to skip second grade. The only other thing I remember clearly about my early school years was that by the time I was in fifth grade, my grades had became deplorable, I believe because my depressing surroundings had caught up with me and affected my schoolwork. Because of the negative atmosphere, it was almost impossible for me to study at home. Things got so bad that I had to repeat fifth grade.

The United States entered World War II in 1941. I remember being at a restaurant and hearing the news about the bombing of Pearl Harbor. Subsequently, our class sold war bonds, but I don't think the war affected me greatly. I had to ride my bicycle to school because gasoline ration coupons were to be used sparingly. And I remember all of us sixth graders being bussed to a hilltop where we were supposed to help level the ground for an army airstrip. Of course I was well suited for that task!

Because my social skills were so stunted, I was very much a loner by the time I started junior high school. I worked hard and gradually started getting better grades. My social life improved along with my self-esteem. Although I didn't have an inkling as to what normal sexual maturing was like, I developed a few childlike crushes. I didn't know how to relate to boys in a romantic way, and couldn't really understand the attraction of dating. I had friends who were boys but no boyfriends until well into my college years.

High school began on a positive note. Although I still performed all the male-oriented tasks at home, I was starting to feel better about myself as a young woman. I enjoyed learning, stimulating conversation, and sports. It's hard to say how things might have turned out, because when I was a junior I had a terrible accident. During a diving lesson, I threw my legs up too far, causing a severe sprain in my back. They said I was unconscious when I hit the water. Due to the sprain, I was forced to spend the next year in bed.

Strangely enough, I loved being the patient for a change. For the first time in my life I was allowed to be weak—to need care and attention. Even though I was sorry to burden my mother with yet another person to care for, I felt like a Queen Bee. Luckily, it was around this time that my father's life insurance finally paid off, making it possible for Mother to hire a maid, laundress, and handyman.

After recovering from the acute stage of my back sprain, I wanted to get my high school diploma and make up for lost time. I completed the second half of my junior year and my senior year all in nine weeks!

College was a real eye-opener for me—socially, emotionally and sexually. I discovered that I was able to get along well with both girls and boys. I found I could carry on highly intelligent conversations and that people actually seemed to like me. Other girls started telling me that I was attractive, and boys started seeking me out. My Puritanical tendencies were still very strong, but for the first time I was beginning to question them. I wanted to be popular and world-wise like the other girls. Most of all I wanted to be well educated so that I could control my own destiny.

Once during the holidays, I brought home a girl I knew from school. My college friends were a very diverse and progressive group. We were kind of an anti-sorority sorority—a clique opposed to cliques. My friend was black, and it never occurred to me that she wouldn't be welcome in our home. But when my mother came to the door she said, "You are welcome home, but THAT will never set foot in this house."

I couldn't believe it! Later I found out that in addition to being racist, my mother was also anti-Semitic and anti-foreign-born. Topics such as politics, race relations, or foreign affairs had simply never been discussed in our home. I felt terribly disappointed in Mother. My friend and I turned on our heels and left. Mother and I never really resolved that issue between us. I knew she would never change, and she never did.

Maybe it somehow runs in the family, but I decided to become a nurse. I excelled at my college studies and maintained a 4.0 grade-point average. With my minor in psychology/sociology, I felt confident that I had found my niche. I was on top of the world.

In 1949 I met the only man in my life who could be both friend and lover to me. It was at a college party. His name was Russell and we were a perfect match. With his craggy good looks, artistic prowess, and extreme intelligence, Russell was the only fellow that made any sense to me whatsoever. He was an "egghead" and liked classical music. We had so much in common. I remember at that first meeting I sat in a chair and Russell sat on the arm of the chair. Totally absorbed in each other, we discussed the deepest of subjects, oblivious to the beer-drinking madness around us.

Russell and I had a fantastic relationship and enjoyed everything together—music, theater, art, philosophy, religion, hiking, roller skating, dinners out, and quiet evenings at his apartment. Through him I learned a lot more about feeling confident about myself as a woman, self-expression, and, yes, sexuality.

I was terribly naive about sex and conception, and still maintained my belief that one had to be married and in a state of "holy bliss" in order to conceive a child. It seems unbelievable to me now that I was so wrongly informed. I was an intelligent young woman, writing articles for a psychology magazine, with an IQ way above average, with this incredible naiveté.

My "belief" was not challenged for more than a year, and Russell and I enjoyed a fulfilling sexual relationship. On New Years Eve 1951 I became pregnant. At first I was elated, thinking that I had achieved that state of "holy bliss." Only it wasn't exactly holy because I wasn't married. And Russell wasn't about to marry me because he was already married to a woman who lived out of town. I had known about Russell's marriage almost since the beginning of our relationship. Maybe I was lying to myself, but his being married never really bothered me—I figured it was his problem.

The thought of telling my mother about being pregnant was horrifying to me. I was afraid of what she might think and do, and I knew it would add to her burdens. I procrastinated as long as possible, and then told her. As I had feared, she was devastated. She insisted I remove myself to a home for unwed mothers in a nearby large city. In 1952 it was not proper for a girl of my class to have an illegitimate baby.

Russell was as adamant as Mother about my giving up the baby. He didn't want any of the complications, commitment, or responsibility. Russell was the only person other than Mother who knew about my pregnancy. The neighbors were told that I had gone off to a private school.

I finished the 1951-1952 college year and immediately moved to the home for unwed mothers. I liked it there. I worked in the office and found the work quite pleasant. Quite easy, in fact. Russell offered to pay my room and board and medical fees, which was decent of him. But when the baby was born, Russell crossed me off his list. I guess he thought he had done his part. He never wanted anything to do with me after that.

Russell was the only man I ever really loved. In my mind, we were the perfect couple. The fact that we would never be married or even be together again had nothing to do with my deep love for him. I know I will carry that love to my grave.

On October 2, 1952, I gave birth to a beautiful little boy whom I named Richard Holbrook Munson. I was allowed to stay with him at the home for one month, and then I was required to hand his tidy little body over to the adoption agency. It was a horrible feeling, letting go of my baby.

I returned home terribly depressed. Russell was becoming more and more distant and had no understanding about my feelings of love and loss for our son. Russell was—and is—extremely self-centered. I was disappointed that he couldn't understand my pain, but I worked hard at trying to forget about it.

Three months later, before the finalizing of my son's adoption, the agency informed me that I could see him one last time. I was overjoyed. I went to the adoption agency and held Ricky in my arms. He was such a special little person. But I knew I was not to be part of his life. I gave him back to the social worker and went home.

Although I was suffering greatly, I began to pick up the pieces and resume my life. The local hospital hired me as an Operating Room Technician due to my excellent grades and high recommendation from the college. I was the first OR Technician in Pennsylvania, and I held that position for three years. Then I met the man who was to become my husband.

Bill was vibrant and fun when I first met him. I was twenty-six, he was twenty-eight—and single. I married him because I thought we had a lot in common. Like me, he enjoyed skiing, camping and hiking, but he wasn't on par with me intellectually. Ironically, it turned out that Bill had experienced a Puritanical upbringing, too. My husband was a very strange man. Conservative and unimaginative, Bill was a "square" and a "workaholic." Though we often disagreed, he never touched me in anger. In fact, he barely touched me much at all. Bill was practically asexual.

Within a year of our marriage, Bill was diagnosed with pernicious anemia, lupus, and diabetes—the same kinds of chronic illnesses that characterized my early life. Isn't it curious how the past revisits us?

Somehow, though, I managed to become pregnant four times. The first two pregnancies ended in miscarriage, which was incredibly sad for me. Then, in 1961, I gave birth to a boy—another Ricky. A little more than I year later I had Brenda.

When the children were ages four and five, it became evident that I was going to have to contribute to the family's income. I applied for a job as a kindergarten teacher. Teachers were scarce then, so I was hired, even though I had no formal teaching training. I was required, however, to complete my bachelor's degree. At the same time, I worked on my master's degree, which I earned summa cum laude.

I loved teaching and felt again like I had come into my own. I was able to combine much of what I'd learned in life with what I'd been taught in school. I felt like I was making an important contribution to society.

Though my marriage was dissatisfying, life was tolerable on the home front. Because of Bill's illnesses, I was in charge of the family. My earlier training as "man of the house" was good preparation, and this time I really enjoyed it—being my own boss in my own home.

I had a secret life, though. I still secretly grieved for my lost son. Every year on his birthday, I would burn a candle and play Ravel's *Pavane for a Lost Child,* a poignantly beautiful piece of classical music. More than a few tears were shed over the years. I worried about my lost son, thought occasionally about looking for him, but had no idea where to begin. My other secret, of course, was that Russell was still the great love of my life.

The 1960s and 1970s passed by and my children were growing up. As I recall, Bill was always either working at the office or sick in bed. His day job was that of a hydraulic engineer. And, since that wasn't enough work for him, he worked evenings for another company as a draftsman. The children didn't see much of him. Like me, they didn't have much in the way of a father figure. We all managed, though. I haven't been particularly close with either of my children, maybe because they've both inherited their father's nose-to-the-grindstone tendencies.

It seems that everything happened in 1980. My son Rick was involved in an automobile accident, and was almost killed when his car broke in half around a telephone pole. Actually, he "died" six times but they "brought him back." He was teaching a friend to drive at the time and nobody knows exactly what happened. The friend survived with only minor injuries, but Rick ended up with two fractured arms, a broken back, a bruised heart, and heaven knows what else. He eventually recovered, but has never seemed the same since. His attitude has turned negative and sour, which isn't conducive to friendship with others or his own happiness.

In December of 1980 several months after Rick's accident, I was alone in the house and the phone rang.

A male voice said, "Shirley? Did your name used to be Shirley Munson?"

"Yes."

"This is Scott Richards."

I had no idea who Scott Richards was, so I said again, "Yes?"

"Tell me, Shirley—what were you doing on the evening of October 2, 1952, at about 6:35 p.m.?"

I could barely speak. "I was having a baby," I finally croaked out.

"Ah! Well, I've changed a lot since you last saw me, Mom. I'm much taller now, and I have a beard."

I tried to picture him, my lost son, tall and with a beard. It suddenly occurred to me how much his voice sounded like Russell's. There were so many emotions jumbled up inside me, it took me awhile to respond. I couldn't get the words out. After what seemed like an hour I said, "Hi, honey. I missed you."

Then the words poured out of both of us. I told him everything. I told him about when he was conceived, and my feelings for his biological father. I held nothing back from him.

Needless to say, I was thrilled. His last name was almost identical to the first name I had given him. We agreed that it was quite a coincidence, and had a long and delightful conversation. I guess you could say we were attempting to catch up on the past twenty-eight years.

There was an instant closeness between us. He told me about his career as a computer consultant. It was a fascinating and high-paying position. He was in the process of writing a book having to do with two of his many passions—travel and computers.

Scott explained that in order to find me, he had first used some notes that were made by his adoptive mother around the time of the adoption. It had taken him a total of three months of casual research, guesswork and cross-correlation to complete the search. After studying telephone directories and making many phone calls, he finally came up with his birth certificate from the state of Pennsylvania. He gave me his adoptive parents' phone number and suggested I give them a call. Then he wanted to know the name of his birthfather.

I gave him Russell's name, and told him the last I had heard, Russell was a jeweler in a town in upstate New York. Later, I found that within minutes of hanging up with me, he was talking to his biological father. This is how that conversation went:

"Hi, Russell. This is Scott Richards. "Tell me—what were you doing on New Years Eve 1951?" Scott just couldn't resist that one.

He discovered that Russell had five other children through five marriages. Like Scott, Russell held art and expression in the highest esteem. Writing and traveling also ran in that family. They made plans to meet in person.

Meanwhile, I called my mother to tell her about Scott's call. By this time Mother had buried all the terminally ill relatives and had moved to Florida to help my sister Muff take care of her children. Ever the caretaker, Mother. Although we had never discussed my baby, Mother's reaction to my son's surprise "appearance" was positive.

Muff had always known about my giving up my baby, though we never discussed it, either. She was very happy for me. Muff and I had developed a good friendship, once we were away from "the Sanitorium." She had built a wonderful life for herself, getting her Ph.D. and becoming an administrator for the Florida public schools.

After that phone conversation, I called Scott's adoptive parents in Ohio and introduced myself. They were both extremely gracious, and expressed a desire to meet me. I let them know that I was interested in meeting them, too.

Scott and I exchanged phone calls for the next few weeks. He flew to upstate New York to meet Russell and his half siblings. Scott eventually developed strong friendships with these people, and now is in regular contact with them. After being raised an only child, Scott suddenly had scores of new relatives. He told me that the first time he met these people, he was amazed because everyone looked like him. Naturally, that had never happened before.

Russell thought it was great to have a ready-made son who appeared at age twenty-eight. No diapers, no adolescent crisis, no requests for money. Scott felt like he was a "chip off the old block," and had inherited Russell's distaste for commitment as well as his characteristic nose and lanky frame.

A few weeks after his meeting with Russell, Scott invited me to visit him in Ohio for five days. Our first meeting was ecstatic. We hugged tightly and then spent the whole afternoon getting to know each other and sharing photo albums. I knew we were soul mates. It was uncanny how much Scott looked and acted like Russell.

That evening when darkness fell, Scott decided to entertain me with his highly technical "laser show" complete with music and special effects. He settled me into a comfortable chair and began preparing the projector and sound system. He told me that the choice of music was critical to the artistic integrity of the show.

The walls and ceiling of Scott's living room came alive with the magic of light. And then, imagine my amazement when the strains of *Pavane for a Lost Child* came to my ears! Although I fought for control over my emotions, I'm afraid I broke down a little. Scott put his arm around me gently.

"Shirley? Do you want me to turn on the lights? Shall I change the music? Are you okay?"

I turned to him and shook my head. "I'm fine. I just wonder how you came to choose this piece of music, that's all."

He said, "I don't know. It's been going through my head all day. I can change it . . ."

Then I told him, "I have played this music every year on your birthday for twenty-eight years, while burning a candle in your memory."

Scott later confided that at that exact moment he actually felt our biological connection.

I also met Pauline and Earl, Scott's adoptive parents, during that first Ohio visit. Wealthy and well educated, his parents were fine people, willing and able to give Scott many advantages I might not have been able to give him. Over the years, Pauline and I became quite close, exchanging letters and phone calls about our thoughts and experiences. Our lives seemed to have progressed in many similar directions.

Earl and I got along well, too. Years later, after both Pauline and Bill had passed away, we still maintained our friendship with letters and telephone calls. Earl recently wanted me to come to Ohio for a visit, but I declined. I am simply not the country club type. Not me. Earl has come out from under the shadow of his wife, who was dominant in their marriage. He is enjoying his life and lady friends.

Bill, Ricky, and Brenda were all happy that I was reunited with my son. Rick and Brenda, both in their twenties at the time, were reasonably excited about having a "new brother." As it ended up, Scott got along better with Brenda than Rick, but that is possibly due to the personality changes from Rick's accident. Scott rarely sees my children, and I don't imagine he'll ever develop very much closeness with them. Too many differences, maybe.

Rick and Brenda have finished college, are married and have children of their own. They are very conservative people—their father's children. They still think Scott is a little odd, and they probably think I am, too.

Scott and I continued our relationship, primarily with phone calls and letters. The next year he came to my home for Thanksgiving. My sister and her children from Florida joined us. We had a delightful family reunion, and Scott keeps touch with his aunt and cousins to this day.

My workaholic husband, Bill, always said his life would be over when he retired at sixty-five, and he was true to his word. He retired from the engineering company, turned sixty-five in May and died in August.

I, on the other hand, have found a certain freedom in retirement and growing older. After teaching for twenty years, I had to retire in 1984 when I had a small stroke. It wasn't serious, thank heavens, but it was just enough to keep me from teaching.

There was plenty to keep me busy, though. When Ricky and his wife were having marital problems, I took their children to live with me for a year, until their parents could begin getting along better. The children were safe and happy with me, and it was nice having young ones around again.

The past revisited again when my mother, aged and ill, came to live in my home for eighteen months. I was nursing my sick husband at the time, too. Knowing the end was near, Mother requested to be put in a nursing home, where she died, quietly and uncomplaining. She didn't want to burden me the way she had been burdened, dear soul.

Several years later I began a little craft business with a friend. It started as a small-time hobby, but has grown to be quite the cottage industry! We make crocheted towels, jackets, and other things and sell them at craft shows and malls in the area. I'm enjoying myself. The handwork keeps me busy, and the craft shows get me out among people.

I have no regrets about my life, and can now look back with happiness and fond memories. I feel immensely proud that Scott, with all his wisdom and intelligence, had the means to cut through the red tape and find me.

Since meeting and knowing Scott, I feel completely fulfilled—a feeling that even eclipses the disappointments of my marriage with Bill. The good things in my life have been enhanced by knowing him, and the negatives have been suppressed. I owe Scott my gratitude for making my life whole again. I thrill in knowing that he is alive and seeing him make a successful life for himself.

I am extremely happy that my continuing love for Russell materialized in our son in such a magical way. As I mentioned before, Russell has always been the only man I've ever loved. Even though Russell wants nothing to do with me, he can't take my love, or the son born of that love, away from me.

The reunion with my son has somehow relieved me of a tremendous inner sorrow. All the years of being told what to do and what to think—coupled with my inability to meet all the unreasonable expectations—left its scars on me. My early training and upbringing shattered my self-confidence. No matter how I fought to regain it, lasting self-confidence always eluded me.

Thanks to Scott's finding me, I've been able to view the past with a saner, more mature perspective. I can finally give myself credit for all that I've done and all that I've become. I have given the earth three very intelligent children and I earned a master's degree cum laude. I am important in my own right—and a free spirit again, after all these years.

Chapter Eight

MY CHILDHOOD WORLD REVOLVED AROUND my mother. As a little girl, I was absolutely devoted to her. I tried to walk like her and talk like her, practicing her mannerisms in front of the mirror. I wanted to be just like Mommy—grown up, poised and in control. I was totally dependent on her, and always was afraid that she would die and leave me and my younger siblings alone with my dad. My dad was an important businessman, had a big scary voice and a mean face, especially when he was drinking.

Mommy always told me "keep all the kids quiet so your dad doesn't get mad." But he seemed to get mad anyway, no matter how hard I tried to keep everything quiet. I hated my dad, but I wanted to please him, too. He hit us kids and at night he would come to me in my bed and hurt me in ways I never talked about. He thought it was funny to have the neighbor boy come over, lie on top of me and move up and down. It still makes me feel sick to my stomach when I think about the things my own father did to me.

My mom needed my dad the way I needed her. She must have, because they divorced and remarried three separate times while I was a child. I don't know if she knew about what he was doing to me, but if she did, maybe that's one reason why she made attempts to get away from him.

Every time he would move out, us kids were so happy, and it was like a weight was lifted from our lives. But then he came back and everything started again. Mom had some physical problems, like migraine headaches and lack of energy. She took pep pills to help her get things done around the house. Sometimes she gave some to me, and I'd stay home from school to help clean. We sure would get a lot accomplished!

When my dad had his after-work drinks, Mom usually joined him. I hated it when she was drunk because her whole personality changed. Usually she was very demure—very private and proper about sexual things. But when she was drinking, she acted all feminine and flirty. I was so embarrassed when she'd go outside and wiggle her hips in front of the neighbor men. Then my dad would get possessive, yell at her to come inside and there'd be a big fight.

My dad was adopted. He complained to me often about how he was a bastard and why his mother gave him up and why didn't she love him. I felt responsible for everything. Though I don't know why, I felt obliged to "keep the monster happy" and I tried to make him feel better, stroking his hand and being nice. In spite of all my efforts, I never felt that my dad approved of me.

In school, I was painfully shy. I went to a large public school in a suburb of Minneapolis. I pretty much stayed by myself and didn't have many friends. After school, I'd hurry home to make sure Mom was still there. There was always a chance she wouldn't be, because sometimes when my dad was away on business or moved out temporarily, Mom would go off somewhere, and not come back for a couple of days. I was afraid she'd go away forever some day. And if she was gone, I had to take care of the younger kids, which made me never want to have children of my own.

I always felt there was something wrong with me, but I never knew what it was. Growing up in the 1950s and 1960s, I believed that most people had perfect families, like the families on television. I knew I had to be perfect if I expected to have a perfect life with Mr. Right. But I knew I wasn't perfect, and I didn't know what to do about it. When I was still in grade school, I was already beginning to experience depression.

Although I managed to develop social skills and had some girl-friends, I was terrified of boys. It seemed like everybody had a boyfriend except me. When I was thirteen, I told my mom, "Eeew! I don't ever want a boy to touch me."

My mom said, "Don't worry. This is just a phase and you'll outgrow it." But when a boy first tried to kiss me, I was disgusted. I became afraid to be in a room alone with a man.

My parents started worrying that I was "abnormal." They took me to a counselor who said I was hypersensitive and had an inferiority complex. Nobody ever mentioned what my dad had done to me, and I had absolutely no memory of it by that time. I had blocked it out.

I hated being young. I wanted to grow up, as quickly as possible. I wanted to get over this silly thing about boys and find Mr. Right. Then I knew I would finally be happy.

Something good did happen during this time, though. When I was fourteen, my parents joined Alcoholics Anonymous. My mom stopped drinking forever, but my dad started again after I became an adult. When my parents quit drinking, life at home became sane for the first time in my life.

Just before I graduated from high school, Mom said to me, "Let's put you on a diet, get you some contact lenses and bleach your hair blonde to get ready for college." I agreed, lost ten pounds and bought some cool new clothes. On the outside I looked like some red-hot mama, but on the inside I was still me. I tried to act normal, though. There were a few casual boyfriends, and I let them kiss me.

In 1966 when I was still eighteen, I met Les at the drive-in. He was a fry cook and I was a carhop. Les was tall, dark and handsome, with a confident swagger and the cutest smile I'd ever seen. I fell in love. Hard.

I wouldn't drink and party like he did. I knew I had to keep my virginity until I was married, so I wouldn't go all the way with Les even though I loved him dearly, with all my heart and soul—with all the feelings I knew I would have for Mr. Right. That's why I could let him touch me. It was two weeks before I was supposed to start college that Les broke up with me because I wouldn't "put out." That's actually what he said to me. I couldn't believe he could be so cruel and leave me like that.

Needless to say, the whole experience with Les made me more confused and depressed than ever. I spent a lot of time crying into my pillow, and threatened to cancel my plans for the university. My mother said, "Don't worry. It'll all turn out for the best."

I was so insecure, in fact, I started to believe that any guy who liked me must be Mr. Right. Lonny was my next candidate. I met him in one of my classes at the university. Almost the first words out of his mouth were, "Would you like to go to homecoming with me?" He was sweet and funny.

Homecoming night, when Lonny asked me what I wanted to drink, I thought, "I'm not going to make the same mistake twice," fearing that I would lose him, too. So I said, "I'll drink whatever you're drinking."

And that was it. I don't remember anything else—what we did, or even if we went to the dance. I think I had sex with Lonny that night but I'm not sure. I just wanted to be loved more than anything in the world. Well, as you might expect, Lonny also dumped me.

I was nineteen and had tremendous guilt about being sexual, but it seemed that since my virginity was gone, there was no reason to stop. Besides, the boys really wanted me to do it. I never really enjoyed sex because I felt too ashamed and too protective of my body to ever have an orgasm. I had to be drunk whenever I had sex. And then afterwards, I'd pretend to myself that I was still a virgin. The doctors had told me I would probably never have children. I only had one or two periods a year and I believed I was sterile.

I started dating Matt, but that didn't last long. One day, Matt and I were at the university coffee shop when in walked Rick, who was gorgeous and dangerous looking. Matt said, "Rick, this is Evie Bennett."

Rick turned his cool glance to me and said, "So what?" From that moment on, I was determined that Rick would be mine. I flirted with him like mad and it finally worked. I stopped seeing Matt when Rick started asking me out. We dated for about a year.

When Rick asked me to marry him, I began to hope again for my perfect life. Since I couldn't have sex unless I was loaded, I don't remember anything about when I got pregnant. After a while I started getting sick. My doctor thought I had ulcers at first.

When I discovered that I was pregnant, I shared this special news with my mom. I was shocked when she started screaming at me—calling me a tramp and a slut. Even though I'd been calling myself those names for a long time, it really hurt to have my mom say them. At the same time, it was almost a relief that she knew the truth about me.

My mom said, "How could you do this? This will break your father's heart!"

I found that pretty hard to believe, but when my mom told him, he actually cried. It's true. Big, sad tears. Watching him, I felt cold and sick inside, like the scum of the earth. I was forbidden to see Rick again, and was shipped off to the San Francisco area to live with friends of my family. I felt afraid. I had never been on my own and away from my mother before. I was horribly lonely and hated having to tell everyone that my husband was away in Vietnam. The only people who knew the real story were my parents, one of my brothers and my best friend. The rest of the people in my life thought I had transferred to a college in California.

Rick wasn't allowed to know where I was, and we had to communicate through letters sent to my dad's Los Angeles office, where they would be forwarded. At least my parents allowed us that contact.

Rick tried to be responsible—he sent me money when he could and even offered to come and get me and try to make it work. I'm afraid I took out my pain and loneliness on Rick, raging at him in my letters. All of this was his fault! I did try to take it easy on my drinking, though, for the baby's sake.

I had to pay a little rent for the room in our friends' house, so I found a series of baby-sitting jobs in different parts of the Bay Area. One of my jobs was in San Jose, baby-sitting for two boys whose mother had died. I commuted almost an hour each way to handle the cooking, cleaning and laundry for the boys and their dad.

One evening as I was getting ready to leave for home, the dad suddenly came out of the bedroom naked. I was shocked. He began saying things like, "Come on, baby, don't play shy with me. We all know what kind of girl you are. You know you want it."

I almost threw up. In fact, I wish I had—all over him. I quit the next day, and found another job.

And here's something else awful—one of my doctors wanted me to sell my baby to one of his other patients for $25,000!

During those months I lived in a nightmare. I felt so guilty about all the pain I was causing my family, Rick, and even my baby. I knew I wasn't cut out to be a mother, and from the moment I discovered I was pregnant, I always knew I would have to give my baby up for adoption—for his own good.

Yet, there was a part of me that absolutely loved, in spite of everything, being pregnant. I loved the feeling of a life inside me, at the same time feeling guilty about being happy. I always felt a strong connection with my baby. I am convinced it is some kind of psychic connection.

Every day I would rub my belly with cocoa butter and talk to him, saying, "You are a special baby and I love you very much. I won't be able to raise you myself, but you will have another mother who will love you. Remember, I will always, always love you. And some day we will come back together again."

I didn't know much in those days, but I knew I would have to say good-bye to my baby—and I knew just as surely that we would meet again some day.

A week before my baby was due, my mom flew out to California to be with me. I ended up being six weeks overdue. Frustrated, the doctor told me I needed to let go of my baby—that I didn't want to give birth to him because I didn't want to lose him.

"You can't keep him inside you forever," he said. "You have to let him go."

I knew that, but my body couldn't do it. My mom and I became closer during that time. I remember we talked a lot and spent quiet times just being together.

When I finally went into labor, I was as big as a house. The birthing process was long and difficult and I lost a great deal of blood. Immediately afterwards I couldn't even stand on my own. Mom had to wheel me down to the nursery so I could see my baby.

But every time I saw him I would start to faint from weakness. I only remember a little red face in a blue blanket and the odor of smelling salts the nurse held under my nose. I never had a chance to hold my baby.

Those two days in the hospital were the most painful days of my life, both physically and emotionally. I was so sore that ice packs and heating lamps were on me most of the time. All I could do was lie there and cry. The nurses had tucked me away in a corner of the ward so I wouldn't upset the other mothers. They were nice enough to put a "Mrs." on my chart, so that nobody would know that I was an unwed mother.

One day a new nurse helped me into the shower, promising to bring my baby as soon as I was finished. I started to cry and told her, "I'm not allowed to see my baby because I'm not married and I'm giving him up." She pulled away from me then, and I slumped to the shower floor and lay there sobbing until I had enough strength to drag myself back to bed.

I tried to imagine raising my son but I couldn't. My father, maybe because of his own feelings of abandonment, wanted me to bring him home. My mother told me if I kept the baby I couldn't come home again. She wanted me to have a better life than she had—an unburdened life. Rick wanted custody, saying his mother would raise the baby, but I couldn't stand his mother and I wanted my baby to have a clean start.

I hated making the decision. It was the most difficult thing I've ever done. But I placed my baby son, whom I named Richard Andrew Bennett, for adoption in November 1968, just two days after his birth. Then I got on the next plane for Minneapolis. I arrived at home sixty pounds heavier than when I had left for "college."

Everything seemed so bleak. I was still a mess physically, too. I stayed in my room for weeks and cried a lot. My mom and dad tried to get me out of my depression, but nothing seemed to work. Except alcohol. That seemed to make me feel better. I tried going out with my old friends, but I felt more distant from them than ever. So I drank even more. I dyed my hair black and started wearing glasses again, trying to make myself as unattractive to men as possible.

In some attempt to put my life back together, I even tried getting together with Rick, but when I called, he wasn't interested in talking to me, having found a new girlfriend.

I eventually got a job as a night manager at a restaurant and lost the extra weight I had been carrying around. I looked great. That was the biggest lie of all because I was such a mess on the inside, starting with the gaping hole that was caused by missing my baby. It was a secret hole and it isolated me from everyone—even myself. Nothing could fill it. Not men, not drugs, not alcohol. But alcohol helped. Or so I thought.

I was on a downhill slide between the ages of twenty and twenty-four. I worked occasionally, went to school from time to time, but I couldn't seem to focus on anything. Due to my ongoing gynecological problems, I started on painkillers—just what I needed! It was also during this time that my parents divorced. Many people started telling me that I was an alcoholic. My girlfriends said I'd get insane when I was drunk and even my doctor was worried I was suicidal and suggested that I had "a problem." One day I couldn't take it any more and called AA, which saved my life.

A few years later, cysts begin to grow on my ovaries. One thing led to another and at twenty-nine, I had to have a hysterectomy. The surgery was awful, but at least I was sober and knew I would be able to have a life afterwards. No more babies, though.

Drunk or sober, I always had trouble with men. I was in therapy pretty much constantly. I guess, when you consider my background, it's only natural that I'd have trouble trusting, fear intimacy, and so forth. I had a lot of short relationships with a lot of men. I got married when I was thirty-five to a sweet guy who was nine years younger than me. Maybe one of the reasons we ended up divorced four years later was that I mothered him. I took care of Johnny totally, even taking responsibility for his emotions. That wasn't a healthy kind of relationship.

Call it intuition or ESP—but I always felt close to my baby, even though we weren't together. And I always knew I would see him again. I remember looking at all the babies at the mall to see if I recognized any of them. For years I looked at all the little boys who were his age. In search of a support system, I called some adoption agencies and located a group of women who had also given their babies up for adoption.

We met regularly, sharing our feelings and experiences. We were also called on to speak to high school and church groups about what unwed pregnancy is really like. That group helped heal my emotional scars more than all the therapy I had undergone over the years.

But I still battled depression. It hit me especially hard at Thanksgiving, which was near his birthday. I put most of my energy into my career and trying to heal, mentally, emotionally and spiritually. I never completely overcame that deep sense of loss, but eventually, I began to believe that I was healthy enough to be reunited with Richard.

When I was forty-three, I began my search for my son by hiring an agency to find him. I began preparing myself emotionally by seeing a counselor who specialized in these things. The counselor also helped me with my feelings about my father. I've made peace with myself over most of it, and the rest I have to just let go. I'm still working on that part.

On August 10, 1992, I had to have my dog put to sleep. As I walked home from the vet's office crying, I said to God, "The only thing that could possibly make me happy today is some news about my son."

I opened my front door and the phone was ringing. The agency had found out who he was! That was when I heard my son's name for the first time—and his last name was almost the same as the first name I had given him! I wrote "Kevin Richardson" in bright blue letters on a piece of paper and hung it on the wall. "This is real," I kept saying to myself. "This is really happening."

The agency promised to send me a copy of his birth certificate and said they'd soon have his telephone number. Holding his birth certificate in my hands, it was so strange, seeing all those statistics that belonged to the two of us—date of birth, time, weight, my doctor's name—but with someone else's names listed as parents. And there I was, crying again. It was hard to believe that I still had tears of grief, considering how much counseling and crying I had been through.

I had to keep reminding myself that I placed him for adoption because it was best for everyone concerned. I do believe that, but it never completely took the pain away. I hung his birth certificate on the wall next to his name and just tried to absorb it all.

About a week later the agency called again to say they didn't know where he was yet, but he had an invalid California drivers license from a few years ago. They told me he was six-foot-two, one hundred eighty-five pounds, had brown hair and green eyes. They told me to be patient. It would be any day now. Each new piece of information I received about him helped me get ready for him. It was very similar to the long labor I had experience twenty-four years before.

I met with an adoption social worker who had dealt with other birthmother-child reunions, and did some reading to help prepare myself. She suggested I write a letter to my son, including all the important things I wanted to say, just in case he didn't want to meet me. I wrote the letter, but I couldn't imagine him not wanting to meet me. I wanted to have the deepest kind of relationship a mother could have with her child.

The morning of October 30, about four months after my initial contact with the agency, they informed me that my son was living in Lincoln, Nebraska. I rehearsed what I would say over and over. The whole day I could think of nothing but that phone call. I decided not to call that day, but to wait until the next, which was Saturday. I couldn't sleep that night. All my fears about being rejected surfaced, and I lay there in the dark, cold and clammy.

I tried meditating to calm my mind and my fears. I kept thinking, "By the end of this day, I will have talked to my son, something I have dreamed about for twenty-four years!" For almost an hour I dialed his number and hung up before it rang. Would he hate me? Would he be angry with me? Would he just hang up and I'd never get to talk to him? Finally, I let it ring. A young woman answered. I asked for Kevin. She said he was at the grocery store and would be back in half an hour. I told her I'd call back. I paced. I cried. I called my friends, my mom, my brother. I thought I was going to hyperventilate, I was so nervous. Then I called my son again.

I said, "Is this Kevin Richardson?"

He said, "Yes."

I said, "Were you born November 24, 1968, in Mountain View, California?"

"Yes, I was."

"Are you adopted?"

"Yes, I am."

As the agency had suggested, I then asked him if this was an okay time for him to take a very personal phone call. He told me it depended on what I had to say. I took a deep breath.

"This is Evie Bennett. I live in Minneapolis, Minnesota. Kevin, I believe I am your birthmother."

A joyful reunion.

There was a long pause and he said, "I've been waiting for this call all my life. What took you so long? Is this really my mom? Are you really my mom?" We talked for about half an hour and spoke to each other every day for a week after that.

When I confided in him that I had been afraid that he might have been angry with me for placing him for adoption, he said, "I always figured that it wasn't a good time in your life to raise a baby and that you loved me so much that you gave me to my mom and dad. Did it happen any other way?"

I told him that was exactly how it was. He suggested that we meet in person—and soon. He wondered what I was doing for Thanksgiving and would it be okay if he and his girlfriend, Maggie, drove up and stay for a few days.

The days and weeks leading up to Thanksgiving were wonderful. We talked almost every day and started discovering similarities. We both use the same slang expressions, we were both allergic to milk, we both had big ears while growing up. He wore his hair short on the sides and a ponytail in the back—just like how I wore my hair. During one conversation he mentioned that his favorite smell was cocoa butter. Cocoa butter! That was what I rubbed on my pregnant belly while talking to him before he was born.

The first picture he sent me went immediately to the photo store where I had eighty copies made to include in the "birth announcements" I sent out to just about everyone I knew.

By the time Kevin and Maggie arrived at my front door, I was a nervous wreck. I hugged Maggie, but my son and I could only stare at each other.

Finally, I gave him a quick hug and said, "Hi."

"Hi," he answered.

We talked about unimportant subjects like movies and the weather. But I couldn't keep my eyes off him. I wanted to take off his shoes and socks to count his toes, just like any new mother, but I had to remind myself that this wouldn't be appropriate.

I wanted to hold him in my arms, tell him a story, rock him to sleep, watch him breathe—everything I didn't get to do before. We stayed up late that night, talking and laughing. We couldn't get enough of each other.

He told me all about his childhood and his family. His life sounded so happy and healthy. Then, he came over to me and held me, as if he were the parent and I the child.

"Thanks for letting me be here," he said.

My counselor had told me that we would go through a period where our bodies would crave each other. She said my body remembers giving him up and his body has a memory of being given up. She said that for a while, until we felt secure that we wouldn't lose each other again, our bodies would need plenty of reassurance.

I don't know if I can describe the feelings I experienced the first time he called me Mom. That was one of the regrets I've had since my hysterectomy—that no one would ever call me Mom. The feeling of being someone's mom was powerful. That Thanksgiving season was the happiest of my life. It was the first time I could wish him "happy birthday" in addition to sharing Thanksgiving dinner with him at my table with the rest of my family.

Meeting my son has changed everything about my life. The secret hole inside is finally filled up—with the love of my son. We've become pretty good about reassuring each other that both of us are here to stay. I feel an inner confidence that I never felt before. I'm sure I did the right thing in giving him up, though. I know I would have been an overprotective, nervous mother. I would have smothered him.

I know I was not cut out to be a full-time mom, but I'm awfully lucky to be able to be a part-time mom. Life is finally okay—in fact, life is something to be excited about. We talk on the phone several times a week and see each other every few months. He is talking about moving to this area to go to school and to live with me, or at least near me.

We are very close. I always knew we were, but at the same time, I couldn't have dreamed that it would be this good. Having Kevin in my life has even helped heal my relationship with his biological father.

My family has accepted Kevin completely. My relationships with men have changed because I'm no longer looking for someone to take care of. I can be a woman with men now, rather than a mother.

There are different reasons for everything now. I still suffer from depression occasionally, but nothing like before I met Kevin. I even enjoy working now because it's fun to work hard, knowing I have my son to buy things for and spoil rotten!

My mother is happy to have Kevin in her life. My sisters and brothers knew about him for years before I found him, and shared my excitement and anticipation. My father is drinking again and I'm mad at him for that. He's only seen my son once so far. I'm afraid that my father is mostly interested in himself.

When Kevin met my mom, sisters, and brothers for the first time he said, "I feel more connected to those people than I ever felt to my own family."

Kevin's family has been wonderful about the whole thing.

The first time I met them they said, "Thank you for our son. We love him very much."

I think his mother is somewhat bothered by our relationship, though. She doesn't want to talk to Kevin about it. On the other hand, Kevin and I talk about everything—we have become so close.

He has a good relationship with his adopted father, and I think that is very healthy. When I went to their house, his father brought out a photo album of Kevin when he was little. A cute little guy! A little later, his mother left the room, came back and handed me a book. It was Kevin's baby book!

It took everything in me not to cry as I slowly read each page. I remembered back to when I was in so much pain about him, and here I was, more than twenty years later, sitting in the home he grew up in, his baby book on my lap, drinking Seven-Up with his parents and finally knowing that everything was fine. No more wondering, no more fear. Just gratitude that he had a good, solid family. And what makes me most grateful of all? That I have my baby back—forever!

Chapter Nine

Julie

I GREW UP IN A SLEEPY LITTLE TOWN in northeastern Vermont, not far from the Canadian border. Born in 1951, I was the eldest of three. My sister, Stephanie, was two years younger than me, and our brother, Joseph, was four years younger. We lived in a small rented house in a quaint little neighborhood, within walking distance of almost everything. I had many friends up and down our street.

It was unusual for mothers to work during the 1950s, but mine did. Mom was a registered nurse in the operating room of a nearby hospital. She was admired by doctors and nurses alike because of her soft-spoken, yet authoritative manner. My dad worked in the car business most of the time, changing jobs often and not making much money, which he blamed on his lack of education. Dad was indecisive, and managed to avoid responsibility by letting Mom handle everything—which she did well. Dad was good at spending money, though, leaving it to Mom to juggle expenses to make ends meet.

Personality-wise, Mom was a stoic, even unfeeling type of parent. As I recall, she never showed much physical attention to me or my siblings, and seldom spoke to any of us at length. I don't remember ever sitting down with her for a mother and daughter chat. She was absent for us, like a ghostly figure who never really revealed herself.

My dad gave us attention, but always in an appraising sort of way. He would remark about how we looked—nice or otherwise. He never kept his comments to himself. If it looked like we had lost or gained weight, he would always let us know. His remarks were particularly painful while I was in my chubby stage.

"Julie is really solid," he'd say, and then invite anyone who was visiting our house to lift me up, like I was a weight to challenge someone's strength.

"Pleasingly plump, isn't she?" he'd chuckle.

Another time when I was playing on the floor with my brother and sister, he said that I was "as broad as a barn door."

He would compare me to my sister who was "thin as a rail."

It was all very hurtful. The three of us children were extremely close. Maybe we banded together because of how we were treated by our parents. We were everything to each other. We were the family. We took care of each other emotionally, being supportive and helping one another through difficult times by telling jokes and laughing.

We thought it was normal that our parents spent all their free time having friends over or going to friends' houses. We though it was normal that our parents consumed a case of beer over a weekend and a couple of six-packs during the week, or even more if there was a party. They were never stumbling, falling-down drunks; they just drank a lot.

We thought it was normal that our parents didn't have much time for us. We were simply not a priority to them. Although we were looked after in terms of food, shelter, and clothing, we felt deprived of their love. Their needs came first.

They both smoked like chimneys, too. I hated it, and told them so. It was horrid to live in a house that was filled with smoke. I was always emptying overflowing ashtrays. My parents didn't care how anyone else felt about their actions—least of all me.

I knew my mother was not happy being married to my father. Dad, although he was never treated for it, suffered from a manic-depressive disorder. His moods could be volatile. He would fly into a rage at the drop of a hat. Mom, usually so cool and level-headed, would respond to his rages by bursting into tears and running to her bedroom. This type of scene was repeated many times throughout our childhood. Of course, there was no explanation to us about what was happening. We just sat there powerless, watching and worrying.

As the oldest child, many things were expected of me. I was house-keeper, cook, and baby-sitter—without pay. I did get to take piano lessons for five years, though, from the nuns at St. Michael's. Whenever I would feel lonely or frustrated, I would play the piano. It was such a great comfort and release for me.

My best childhood memories involve my grandparents. I was very close to all four of them. I knew they liked having me visit at their homes. My mother's parents in particular, made me feel wonderful. They lived about twenty miles from us in a rural dairy community in a weathered old country home with a veranda that wrapped all around the house. Grandfather had been a blacksmith and Grandmother had stayed home to raise six children. They were the soul of love and solid character.

I remember spending hours in the garden with Grandfather. I felt so small among the looming rows of corn. I can still smell the ripe tomatoes. His crops were always magnificent. We would pick the vegetables and carry them in a bushel basket to Grandmother, who always seemed to be in the kitchen.

I loved watching Grandmother work. She used the same big blue bowl and the same utensils every day. She was methodical as she pared the potatoes and prepared the rest of the meal. I was mesmerized by her ritual movements around the kitchen. It was like a beautiful and graceful dance.

After lunch we would play checkers, cards, or Scrabble. They never rushed. I felt such joy at being with these two people who had all the time in the world—just for me.

Grade school was difficult for me at first. I was a very chubby child, and kids love to torment anyone who is different. After the others got to know me, though, I ended up having a large circle of friends. I knew I was well liked, which gave me confidence. I was voted president of my class every year. The teachers always loved me. They knew they could depend on me to take charge of the class or do any extra work that needed to be done. I enjoyed the attention and the role of leader.

When I was thirteen, my parents bought the only house we ever owned. It was right across the street from our old rented house, and like a dream come true for me. The new house was a huge Victorian-style, with ten big rooms and two bathrooms.

The wealthy man who had owned the house left us some of the furnishings. There were beautifully ornamented lamps and antique handcrafted wooden furniture. The small lot was professionally landscaped with trees, shrubs, and a lovely rose garden in back. I had never known such grandeur. That house made me very happy.

About a year later, in 1965, I started changing physically, and the changes were quite rapid. I grew taller, lost my chubby shape and became a well-developed, attractive teenager. I had shoulder-length brown hair with red highlights. Every night I set my hair in those huge rollers we used in those days, to take out its natural wave, because the straight look was popular then. I wore only a little mascara. I really didn't need much makeup. I had one of those peaches-and-cream complexions, except in summer when I'd get freckles.

In high school, people thought I had a great smile. Those teen years were wonderful. I was on the student council, played basketball and sang in the choir. It was the first time in my life that I felt good about how I looked. The boys took notice of me right away. I couldn't get enough attention or compliments. I felt a sense of power. I had a feeling of self-worth that I had never experienced before.

Since my parents had never talked with me much about anything, of course they never talked to me about sex. Mom seemed quite concerned when I started dating, but she never gave me information about the feelings that can happen between a boy and a girl. Nor did she inform me about contraception. I guess she believed that I would just somehow be a "good girl."

She didn't know that I had been involved in some fairly heavy petting from about eighth grade on. I was happy with just petting, and assumed my boyfriends were, too. When I was fifteen, I started being pursued by Jim, who was a senior. Although his brazen behavior and public show of interest in me were a little intimidating, I was flattered by the attention. I liked what I thought were decision making skills and strong work ethic. I thought he was sensible and stable. After about five months of dating, Jim demanded that we have sex, threatening to leave me if I refused. I couldn't face the thought of life without him, so I reluctantly gave in.

We were lucky for a year, but in late June of 1967, I realized I was pregnant. I couldn't believe this was happening to me. I was on the student council and the basketball team. I wanted to go to college and become a teacher. Instead, it was all over for me, that summer before the start of my junior year. I tried not to think about it.

Jim had graduated and was signed up to enter the Navy in August. I remember the evening I told Jim about my condition. We were watching the movie *Alfie* at our local theater when I started to cry. Jim asked me why I was crying and I said, "Because I'm pregnant!"

We left the theater and went to have Cokes and talk about it. Neither of us had any idea of what to do. So we did nothing. He left for the Navy, and I got ready to start school.

I didn't look pregnant, and even though I was sick every morning getting ready for school, I just pushed it all to the back of my mind and pretended that none of it was happening.

When I was about five months along, my clothes started fitting a little snugly. One Saturday before my dad came home from work, I walked into the kitchen and found Mom sitting at the kitchen table, as if she had been waiting for me.

When she blurted out something about my not having a period and could I be pregnant, I replied, "Yes."

She started crying and saying hurtful things like, "We never thought that you, the perfect student, the good child, would end up like this!"

Then she dropped the bombshell, telling me that I had been born out of wedlock. I couldn't believe it. She had been twenty-one years old and Dad had been in the service. I also found out that my mother didn't even raise me for the first two years of my life—I had lived with her parents until Dad got out of the service. All of a sudden, I understood why I had always felt such a sense of closeness to those grandparents.

As if that wasn't enough, she went on to tell me another family secret. My dad's sister had given birth to an illegitimate child and placed him for adoption. My mom sure chose a great time to tell me all of that.

When she was finished with me, I was overwhelmed. I left the house and started walking toward our church, which was a block away. I was a devout Catholic, and felt the need to go to confession, to confess my sin.

The priest was so kind and understanding. He made me feel much better. As I was on my way back home, I noticed that my dad was walking toward the church looking for me. He came up to me and just hugged me. He didn't say a word. Somehow, he must have known how I needed that. Without talking, he had finally let me know that he loved me.

I didn't know it at the time, but the priest's kind reaction and Dad's unspoken love would have to hold me for a long, long time.

My mother took me to the family doctor, I think with the idea of abortion in mind. The doctor said it was too late—that I was three month pregnant. Too far gone. The doctor was wrong—I was five months along. But what difference did it make?

Mom and Dad put their heads together and decided to send me off to live with my aunt. When that plan fell through, they came up with another. At 11:00 P.M. one night, Dad woke me up to tell me that all of us except him would be moving to Arizona. We would stay with my uncle until after I had the baby.

My opinion was never sought in any of this planning. No one asked me how I felt about these decisions. But at that point, I was relieved that someone else was handling the problem.

In November of 1967, Mom, Joseph, Stephanie, and I began our drive from Vermont to Arizona. We told everyone that my parents were having marital problems and they were separating for a while. Other than our immediate family, nobody knew the real truth. My boyfriend, Jim, didn't tell his family. I never told even one friend.

I was confused, frightened and worried. What would happen to my body during the pregnancy and labor? What about afterwards—what would my body be like when it was over? Where would I go to school? Where would we live? What would happen to my child?

Mom never talked about any of this with me, and I was too ashamed to ask. I felt bad for letting myself get into this predicament. I should have been smarter. I felt guilty for putting my brother and sister through the trauma of moving away from our lovely home. I felt awful about all the arrangements my parents had to make financially, and for Mom having to quit her job. Most of all, I felt so alone!

We arrived at my uncle's home in Tucson tired and irritable. He lived in a fairly large house with his wife and eight children. It was the first time we had met our cousins. They were not very friendly to us, so there was no companionship to be found there. With four more people, the house was crowded, too. But the worst part was that no one ever mentioned my condition.

It didn't take Mom long to find a job in a nearby hospital. She located an apartment and enrolled us in school. Coming from a small town, I found the high school intimidating. It was the size of a college campus! Kids from our part of the city had to begin classes at 6:00 A.M. My mother formed a car pool with other parents in our apartment complex and they took turns driving us to and from school. I was exhausted by the time I got home from classes at 12:30. All I could do was drop into bed for a nap.

I was expanding quickly and had no maternity clothes, so I wore a trench coat to school in an attempt to hide my condition. Fortunately, baggy dresses were in style, so I still had a few clothes that fit, but I was running out of things to wear and Mom didn't seem to care.

In December, Dad came from Vermont for a Christmas get-together. It was really nice to see him. I was almost eight months pregnant and Mom had finally bought me two maternity outfits. That was all I had to wear. Mom seemed happier while Dad was there. It was a strange Christmas, but good to be together again.

One day, within weeks of when I was due to deliver, I was called into the principal's office and told that I was expelled from school for being pregnant. Pregnant girls were not allowed in school, and I was to call my mother to come get me.

I was so humiliated and was in tears when Mom arrived. She took me home without a word of comfort. Just her cold silence, as always. The following week she took me to a special school for unwed mothers. Even though I ended up only being there for two weeks, it was the one place I felt I belonged. The other girls and I were all going through the same thing, and that felt comfortable. Plus, classes were held at a reasonable hour, so I didn't have to get up so early.

It was January before Mom took me to a doctor again. Even though she was a registered nurse, she had not taken me for any prenatal care. The doctor examined me, then admonished me for putting my family through this ordeal. There were no words of consolation. He acted as if I had the plague, muttering something about why is it that the pretty and smart girls always seem to end up like this. I hated the man.

One day in February, although I wasn't sure at first, my labor started. I had spent many hours in the school library trying to learn about labor and delivery, so I had gained a little knowledge. Neither my doctor nor my mother told me anything about what to expect. I didn't tell Mom about the pains when she left for work at 2:30 that afternoon. But by 7:30 I had to have Stephanie call Mom and ask her to come home.

Mom arrived home, a little upset because I hadn't mentioned anything to her before she had left for work. Off we went to the hospital—a different one than the hospital where Mom worked. I don't remember Mom saying good-bye to me at the hospital. I just remember her being gone. I guess she went back to work.

They took me to a labor room and the pains began in earnest. I remember thinking how unpleasant and painful it all was. By about 9:30 P.M. my doctor arrived and broke my water. Then things went really fast, and the pain became intense. There was no sympathy or encouragement from anyone. I don't believe the doctor even spoke to me. Once, when I moaned aloud in pain, the nurse scolded me, saying, "All that noise won't make the pain any easier, you know."

At about 10:00 P.M. I was taken to the delivery room. A mask was placed over my face and everything went dark. When I awoke, I was in a private room in the hospital. Mom was standing nearby looking worried, but I don't remember her saying a word to me.

I was not allowed to see my baby. The nurses wouldn't even tell me if I had a girl or a boy. Finally, the next day, the doctor told me that I had a son who weighed seven pounds, one ounce. That's all I knew about him for twenty-five years.

My parents made the decision that my son would be adopted by a loving, two-parent family. That was it—no discussion. I was seventeen, and had been told that I could not finish school while raising a child, so it seemed for the best. At the time, I had no idea how losing my child would impact the rest of my life.

After signing papers in the hospital, I cried and cried. A nurse came in and whisked my mother out of the room, saying I needed time alone. Again, no one was there to comfort me. I left the hospital the next day, and two weeks later we were all on our way back to Vermont.

I felt empty. I felt as if I had left part of myself in Arizona. I had no one to talk to about this, because no one outside the family knew, and no one in the family would even discuss it. I couldn't even talk to Stephanie about it. We had always talked about everything, but the whole subject became taboo to even think about, much less talk about.

I went back to my old high school three months before the end of the school year and graduated the following year. It was a time of emptiness and loneliness. My whole attitude about life had changed. I was no longer interested in anything—not even basketball. The spirit that had made me a leader was gone. I floated along in kind of a dream state.

Jim was still in the service while I was finishing high school, so I took advantage of his absence to date other people. I was horrified by the changes the pregnancy had caused to my body. It was obvious that I would never be the same again. I had been so proud of my body just two years before, but now I viewed myself with loathing and disgust. Attention from males helped me feel better about myself. I wasn't promiscuous, but I needed men to be sexually attracted to me in order to feel whole.

Even though my parents had forbidden me to see him, Jim and I started dating again when he was discharged from the Navy. After a time, he even came to my house to ask my parents' permission to date me again. I always admired this forthright quality in him. My parents eventually relented.

Jim and I started having sex again, still without contraception. I have no idea why we ventured into those dangerous waters again. After a few "false alarms," during which I became very panicky, we decided we should get married, and became formally engaged. I felt like I had to stay with Jim because he was the father of my child. He was the only bond I had with my son.

Because our family didn't have enough money for me to go to college, I opted for a two-year medical secretary course. After graduation, I commuted to classes, not wanting to live on campus because I didn't want to be apart from Jim. I knew I would be tempted to see other men if I stayed on campus. As it happened, I did see other men, but I never pursued anything long term with any of them.

Jim and I married in 1971, three years after our first son was born. I always felt as though something was missing from our relationship. Nevertheless, after three years of marriage, we decided to start a family. Daughter Kim was born in 1975 when I was twenty-four, and about three years later we had our son Jamie. The children helped fill the void in my life, and heaven knows, they kept me busy.

While I was on maternity leave with Kim, I saw a Phil Donohue show about adoptees who were searching for their birthparents. Something about that show convinced me that I would find my son. I wanted desperately to let him know that he had always been loved. I contacted a search organization, paid a membership fee and received a very skimpy guide about how to conduct a search. I tried to read it but got confused. I put the guide away, and didn't do anything else about it for years.

My marriage was not very satisfying for me. Jim worked endless hours and was rarely home to help with the kids. It was frustrating to work full time myself, and then come to home to the burden of raising children alone and keeping house. I sometimes thought I would go over the edge.

While I was pregnant with Jamie, Mom was living with us temporarily. She was dying of lung cancer. During my entire pregnancy, she was receiving radiation treatments and declining rapidly. It was a lot of extra work for me, but I figured it was my duty to take care of her. My mother died when Jamie was eight months old. It was a terribly depressing time. Mom and I never did manage to discuss my first son's birth or any of what had happened. Now we will never be able to discuss anything.

The next year, Dad lost his job. He and Mom had been separated since she got sick, and he'd been drinking very heavily. He was only in his early fifties at the time, but he never worked again. I believe he eventually quit drinking, but his severe depression and self-centered attitude keep us apart to this day. He only wants to talk about himself. It is nearly impossible to have a two-way conversation with him. Dad and I rarely see each other, and he's really not a part of my life.

There were many times when I thought I should leave my husband. He had become very much like my father, with uncontrolled mood swings and depression. I hated the mind games he kept playing. There were times he would refuse to talk to me. Once, three months went by without him speaking to me. But I didn't have the courage to leave Jim. I wasn't financially secure and didn't want to be poor, so I stayed. We tried counseling, but he never believed that he had a problem. He said any problems we had were mine.

By 1990, things got really bad. The business that Jim and his brother-in-law owned burned to the ground. We went through a dreadful time, suing the insurance company, and then never recovering the money we should have. Jim had to get a job at two-thirds of his former salary, and our lifestyle changed dramatically. He became even more depressed, and so did I.

I sought counseling for myself, which began a two-year period of working through my issues, especially the birth and loss of my first son. Jim never seemed to share my deep feelings about our son. This was the first time I had been able to explain my sadness to someone who understood, and it took so much energy to bring all that out of me.

In time, I went from individual counseling to a group with four other women. I was finally able to tell my story and hear people's reactions. I started to feel like I was recovering and finding myself again. Since 1992, I've continued to come to terms with my losses. I have learned how to grieve and then move on.

I never stopped thinking about my first son. I think the healing I experienced in counseling gave me the strength to start my search. I wrote for the hospital records and found the name of the lawyer who had handled the adoption. When I wrote to him, I received a curt reply that he had died. When I wrote asking what had become of the records, I was told they'd been destroyed. I contacted the lawyer's wife to see if she could help, but a secretary wrote back saying not to bother her with this. I later found out that this lawyer had been my first son's godfather.

I was stymied. I found out about another search organization, and located a contact person in Arizona. This woman worked in a state office and had access to adoption records in a card file. When I called her she was able to get the information in front of her, but said that she couldn't tell me anything. She did tell me that his name was Kenneth. That was something, at least. I finally had a name to call my son.

Several months and many phone calls later, she mailed me some non-identifying information. I received the package at work and almost collapsed when I opened it. What a joyful surprise. There were four photos of Kenneth when he was little. Now I had a face to put with the name. There in front of me, in these pictures, was my son.

I called Jim at work to tell him, but couldn't even speak through my tears. I tried to express the happiness and relief I felt just at seeing those pictures. I didn't feel like Jim understood, but I think he was happy for me.

Another search group in Phoenix helped with the remainder of the process of finding my son. There were many layers of information to uncover and piece together. My sister and I spent many hours at libraries going through various documents. We ended up finding Kenneth's family through names of men in northern Arizona who were connected to a particular church. Searching the church records, we found a man and his wife with a son named Kenneth who was born in 1968. Bingo!

I was almost positive that this was my son—but how to make contact? I was going to write a letter, but my search team suggested that a phone call would be best. They were right. After all this searching, I really needed to know—now.

On May 7, 1993, at about 9:15 P.M. Eastern Time, I called the Arizona phone number where I thought Kenneth lived. A woman answered. That threw me—I was expecting him to answer. She sounded older, so it probably wasn't his wife. I assumed it was his adoptive mother.

"My name is Julie O'Grady," I told her. "I gave birth to your son Kenneth in 1968."

She sort of gasped, but then began to thank me for giving them such a wonderful son—going on and on about what a great guy he was, so articulate and what gorgeous eyes he had. I asked her some questions, especially about what he looked like now, since the only pictures I'd seen were when he was little.

She described him to me. She said Kenneth was twenty-five years old, six feet tall, had bluish-gray eyes, blonde hair and had graduated from a college in California with a degree in history and video production. I asked as many questions as I dared, then asked where he lived. She wouldn't tell me or give me his phone number. But she promised to contact him and let him know I wanted to speak with him. I also made her promise she wouldn't leave me dangling for days—that if he didn't want to talk to me, she'd call me right away.

Kenneth called the next day. It was the day before Mother's Day. His voice sounded very gentle and low, and there was a degree of excitement in it, too. I started to cry, so I asked him to please give me a couple of minutes to collect myself. Then we talked for about thirty minutes. I told him about his family in Vermont, the circumstances of his being adopted, and how I found him.

He was amazed at all I had gone through to find him. He had thought of searching too, but had no idea where to start. He also wanted to make sure that I had the right person. That made me chuckle. I knew he was my son.

Kenneth told me that he lived in Chicago now, and his main occupation was playing in a heavy metal-type band called "Angst." His dream was to make it big time in the music world. In the meantime, he was supplementing his income as a bar manager at a downtown cafe. I thought it a little strange that his adoptive mother never mentioned the band.

Kenneth went on to say that the band might be playing in New York that July, and maybe we could meet then. I was excited and frightened. Would he like me? What kinds of things would I find out about him when I actually got to know him?

I needn't have worried, because that meeting never happened. The band didn't get the job in New York. Time just kept rolling by with very little contact initiated by Kenneth. In the past few years I have received maybe three letters and two phone calls. The rest of the time I have done the contacting.

My family was happy to hear I had found my son. Jamie, who was sixteen, was most enthusiastic about having an older brother. Kim, however, wasn't as excited and told Jamie that she couldn't picture Ken as part of our family, and that he would never be a real brother to Jamie. Jim was quietly supportive, but had no desire to speak with Ken on the phone or write to him. I couldn't quite understand that, since Jim was his father.

In the summer of 1994, I decided that the only way to have closure to my search was to see him in person. He clearly had no intention of making a trip to Vermont, even if I sent him an airline ticket. So I asked if we could come visit him. I was a little surprised that he seemed excited about the idea.

On October 5, 1994, my sister, Stephanie, my son, Jamie, and I made the trip to Chicago to meet Ken. He and his girlfriend, Tessie, were right at the bottom of the ramp as we came off the plane. There was no time to put down our bags and take a photo, but the picture of his face at that moment is indelibly printed in my mind.

My first feelings were a little odd. Here was my son, my child, a stranger. He seemed shorter than I had imagined him, but so beautiful. His gentleness and nervousness were evident as we left the airport and drove into the city. I kept trying to memorize everything about him, without letting him know that I was staring. I'm sure I was not as discrete as I tried to be. He dropped us off at our hotel and then went home to change for dinner. I think he just needed a little time away from the intensity of the situation.

Ken had a hard time relaxing with us. He seemed most comfortable the day before we left, when the two of us were going through the family photo album I had brought along for him. It was an emotional three days, and I was a little frustrated that we didn't have as much time together as I had hoped. He had to work all day Friday, and edit a video with the band at night. After traveling so far, I got to see him so little. And I was still unable to get him to commit to a Vermont visit.

I had fantasized that this meeting would help integrate Kenneth into our lives, and that contact with him would be more ongoing. But it hasn't happened that way. Ken told me that he needed space to sort out his feelings about being found, and he wanted me to be patient with him. I was trying to be patient, but I desperately wanted him as part of my family. He was my son.

I sent Kenneth's adoptive mother, Sharon, a short letter, telling her how fortunate Ken was to have been placed in such a warm family, and that he had told me many good things about her. I invited her to get to know me and ask me questions if she wanted. I said that I hoped we would get to know each other and maybe be friends some day. I received no response to that letter.

At Christmas, I sent another card and letter, telling her that I understood if she was uneasy about all of this, but assured her that we only wanted to give Kenneth our love, and in no way meant to usurp her position as his parent. Again, no response.

I knew that Ken's adoptive parents had divorced about a year before, so I assumed Sharon was going through some emotional upheaval. I thought I'd try the adoptive father. I sent him a letter with similar messages. No response from him, either.

This made me angry. What could they possibly fear from me? I lived twelve hundred miles from Kenneth and twice as far from them. I had no power to undo the past—no power to threaten their parental roles. But apparently, they had no desire to know me or my family. I gave them my child and they refused to even acknowledge me.

Meanwhile, life went on. Jim was in the car business, which he hated. Ironically, he worked at the same job my father had. Jim was frustrated and depressed a lot of the time. Our relationship was far from perfect. It was difficult to find a common ground, as he didn't share many of my interests. But our marriage was not completely negative by any means. Jim always tried to be a good husband and provider. And I had to own part of our problems as well. The experience of losing Kenneth made me a different person than I would have been, and I had my own demons to deal with around that issue. I knew I had not always been the easiest person to live with.

I continue to work at the university as a technical secretary in the medical field—at the same type of job I've had since my marriage. Because of the tuition remission policy, I've been able to afford college educations for Kim and Jamie. My work isn't very challenging, but I've been taking classes with the goal of finishing my four-year degree. I'm not sure where this will take me, but I've always wanted to teach—maybe in adult education.

It was only after finding my son that I was able to progress with my ambitions. I am regaining the confidence I lost so long ago, and can pursue my own dreams. The whole search experience set me free from the dark hole I had been buried in. It has been an emotional cleansing. I feel more secure about myself now, and am slowly getting rid of the guilt about the past. I am feeling less like a teenage girl who shamed her family, and more like the strong and worthwhile woman I am.

There are still many unanswered questions where Ken is concerned. He has become a kind of obsession with me. I think about him and worry about him every day. I wonder what he is feeling about me. I have decided that this compulsive behavior needs to stop. I need to stop getting bogged down with worrying about what he will or will not do about our relationship.

I will never abandon him again, but I need to have a clear space in my mind. I need to let him go and decide for himself if he wants to be part of our lives.

Painful as it is, I have decided not to initiate further contact with my son. I can't be the only person in the relationship willing to make a commitment. I will send gifts and a letter on Christmas and his birthday, but will not try to force anything. I can't have this relationship alone. He needs to want me, too. No matter how long it takes, I will continue to wait for him.

Chapter Ten

Bonnie

*O*UR FAMILY WAS SOUTHERN through and through—from the depth of our religious convictions to the height of our moral standards. We were Mother, my brother Paul, Daddy, and me. A completely traditional family, we went to church not once, but three times a week. Daddy was a Baptist deacon and both my parents were Sunday school teachers. I liked going to church when I was little because I could get dressed up in one of my many frilly dresses. I was one of the best-dressed girls in town, and I had perfect attendance at Sunday school for seven years. It's true that I came from a good home, but perhaps I was too sheltered and given too much.

We lived in a small town just outside of Atlanta, Georgia, which wasn't the big city it is today. In the 1950s and 1960s there were no interstate highways, and a shopping trip into Atlanta was always a big event.

Daddy was a railroad conductor. His usual route was between Atlanta and Chattanooga and he rode the train's caboose. The tracks were across the road from our house. When his train would come by I'd shout, "Here comes Daddy's train!" Then we'd all run out to the front porch to wave. I was allowed to ride on the train for free any time I wished. It was so much fun!

The people in Daddy's family were all pillars of the community, but Mother's relations apparently were not. My mother's parents lived with us.

"Papa" was a diabetic with an artificial leg, which fascinated me. He was sort of emotional and would cry sometimes when he talked about his mother. As a young woman, his mother lived in a small shack in the mountains of West Virginia and worked hard to raise her five children.

She "took sick" and died when Papa was about ten, leaving his father to tend to the family. Papa was forced to go to work. Because of his early responsibilities, Papa only had a few years of "schooling" and only learned to read a little when he was in the Army. He was very embarrassed about this and blamed his lack of education for his lack of job opportunities.

"Mama" had had a rough childhood, too. At age eleven she went to work in a textile factory. She was so small that she had to stand on a stool to reach the large spools of thread. Needless to say, this was all before the child labor laws.

Mama liked to "dip" snuff. She always kept a tin can nearby—her "spit can." Her sisters and Papa's brothers all either dipped or chewed tobacco. One weekend when I was about five, my great aunts and great uncles were visiting at our house. This was probably 1954, and playing "Cowboys and Indians" was all the rage. My brother Paul and I wanted to make "Indian arrows" so we sneaked out to the chicken coop to pull feathers from one of our sitting hens (we let the hens sit on their eggs when we wanted baby chicks.) I didn't realize it, but on one side of the pen was a huge wasp nest. I popped my head right into it and before I knew it, I was covered with wasps!

Screaming, I ran to Mama and the rest of the old folks on the porch. Do you know what they did to treat my stings? Spit tobacco juice all over me! I couldn't believe they were doing this, but it worked. Who knows—that home remedy might have saved my life.

Paul and I loved Mama and Papa with all our hearts and souls, and we knew they loved us, too. But Mother always told these unbelievable tales about them having been abusive alcoholics. She told us about how she and her sister were "good girls from a bad home." According to Mother, Papa would work every day but then he'd drink from Friday night straight through Sunday. She said Mama drank with him and they'd have huge fights. Mother said Papa even chased Mama around the house shooting a gun! It was hard for us to believe these things, because they were nothing but sweet to us. Anyway, as my grandparents aged, Papa's health problems set in and they didn't have much money. When they asked Mother if they could live with us she said they could, as long as there was no alcohol in the house. And nobody ever did bring alcohol into that house. Never.

Daddy (I still call him Daddy) and I have always been very close. I remember sitting on his lap, prattling on about every little thing that had happened to me that day, and him just listening. He would smile, stroke my head and listen.

I think Mother was jealous of my closeness with Daddy. She liked my brother best, though, and that was obvious to me. She always seemed to have time to talk to him. Mother had health problems and was sick off and on from the time I was a baby. At first they thought she had cancer but it was actually some other type of inoperable growth which collapsed one of her lungs.

With her respiratory and heart problems Mother couldn't handle housework but she was able to work as a secretary. She tired easily and was often worn out when she came home at night. I don't think she ever had much time or energy to be with me.

I loved and admired my big brother, Paul, who was eight years older than me. He was very talented musically and extremely popular. I couldn't wait to get older. I remember wishing my childhood would end so I could go to high school and be just like him.

As luck would have it, I ended up hating high school. In 1963 when I started ninth grade the Atlanta district lines were changed and I was separated from most of my friends. Also, the school system in the south was not exactly the greatest. I was an intelligent kid and I felt like I was wasting my time in school, having already learned most of what was presented. I started playing hooky a lot, and hanging around with older kids—mostly older boys.

As you might expect, sex was not a subject of discussion in my family. It was pretty much treated as if it didn't exist, except within the sanctity of marriage. Mother did prepare me for having my period by giving me only the basic facts. One of my most vivid memories about Mother's guidance was when I was about fourteen. She told me how proud she was to have kept herself "pure," and how wonderful it is on your wedding night to have saved yourself for your husband.

When I brought up the subject of premarital sex, Mother said, "I would rather see you dead than pregnant before you get married." Believe me, I never forgot that statement.

A horrible thing happened when I was thirteen. I found out that my brother "had to get married." He didn't tell my parents that his fiancée was pregnant, though. They never knew about it until after the baby was born. At first they thought my nephew was born early—at six months! But then Paul confessed and, after the initial shock, the subject was never mentioned again.

Maybe if I'd been satisfied in school things might have turned out differently for me, but I guess we'll never know. When I was fifteen I became romantically involved with B.J., an eighteen-year-old college student. In truth, he had been my sweetheart since I was about eleven. We used to meet behind the schoolhouse and kiss, but we didn't actually date until I was fifteen.

I thought myself quite mature, and we eventually started having sex. I felt happy and guilty at the same time. This relationship with "an older man" distanced me from my classmates and made me think of myself as older than them. When I was sixteen, B.J. became a part-time student with a full-time job. Because this was 1965 and the war in Vietnam was heating up, he was drafted almost immediately. I wanted desperately for him to marry me, but he said I'd have to wait until he got home.

I'm ashamed to admit it now, but I was very angry at him. "What?" I exclaimed. "You want me to wait a whole year to get married? You must be kidding!"

We had a big, ugly fight and broke up. Then he was shipped overseas.

I felt completely alone in the world after B.J. left. Mother and Daddy must have been concerned about me, but I was too involved in my own problems to notice. I didn't feel like a teenager, but I knew I wasn't an adult, either. I couldn't relate to the few friends I had.

One night I went to a teen dance with my friends and in walked Jimmy Paulson, the handsomest hunk of man I'd ever seen. I think my heart actually skipped a beat when he asked me to dance. We danced to a few songs and then went out to his car where we talked and listened to music. He had a funny sense of humor and made me feel like I was his equal, even though I was sixteen and he was twenty-two.

For the next year or so we dated—dinner and the movies, most often the drive-in movies, where we petted heavily, and eventually went "all the way." During this time he had met my family and even joined us for Sunday dinners. Mother and Daddy approved of him. They never suspected what we were doing. Sometimes I'd sneak off to meet him at night when my parents were asleep. We were terribly in love. Everything was great, but all good things must come to an end, right? One night the condom slipped off.

I had assumed that we would marry when I finished high school. Then when I was pretty sure I was pregnant, I thought we'd go ahead and marry right away. When I told him I was pregnant, he became very sad and apologetic. Tears came to his eyes and he said, "I am so sorry for what I've done to you."

It didn't matter if he was really sorry or not. Turns out, his name wasn't even Jimmy. His name was Billy—and he was already married! What's more, his wife was pregnant, too! Our relationship came to a screeching halt.

Looking back on it, I don't want to judge Jimmy/Billy too harshly. He was hurt by the situation and after all, a lot of people do things they shouldn't.

But then, my whole world felt suddenly blown apart. The man I loved was not even who I thought he was. Everything had been a lie.

I can barely remember anything about the first few months of my pregnancy. I think I was in shock. I didn't know what to do. I had some crazy thoughts. I pretended none of it was true—that everything would go away if I pretended hard enough.

I thought about having an abortion but didn't know where or how to find out about such a thing. I thought I would run away to California where my cousin Annie lived. Maybe she would help me. I even made plane reservations. But my parents somehow found out that I was planning to run away. That's when they confronted me about my "weight gain."

I was five and one-half months along and, of course, would not have approached my mother with the news, given her earlier comment about rather seeing me dead than pregnant. When my parents did find out, such a look of sadness came over Daddy's face. And then he cried. I did not ever see him cry before. That sad look never went away, and I was never able to look him straight in the eye after that day. I still can't. Mother was near tears, too, and shaking. I remember being afraid she'd have a heart attack, given her already bad health.

But Mother somehow pulled herself together and took the bull by the horns. She had read about maternity homes in a "Dear Abby" column and called the one closest to Atlanta. It was full and there was a long waiting list. I had no idea there were so many girls who had gotten in trouble. Mother was anxious to get me somewhere where I could get professional help. She and Daddy thought I was near some type of breakdown and maybe I was.

Another really sad thing happened during this time. My old boyfriend B.J. came back from Vietnam on a thirty-day leave and appeared at our door one day. He said he still cared for me and wondered if we could get back together again. I had to tell him that I was pregnant—with another man's baby. He was devastated and I felt even more guilty than before.

I didn't tell anybody who the father of my baby was. Daddy kept pressuring me to tell him but I was afraid he'd go and kill Jimmy/Billy if he knew what he had done to me.

Mother suddenly became very involved in my life. She was terrified that Daddy's family would find out about my pregnancy, so she concocted a story about my having quit school and accepted a job in another town, where I was living in a woman's boarding house. She must have been a really good liar because nobody—not even my brother or Mama and Papa—guessed at the real story. To them, I had simply gone off on vacation with my parents, found a job and didn't come home for several months. Everybody bought it. At least I think they did.

I arrived at the home in Tennessee July 7, 1967, the day after my eighteenth birthday. I was six months pregnant and, with the help of a tight girdle, had successfully hidden my condition from virtually every-one.

I was advised that during my stay, I could use either my real first name or an alias, if I preferred. The girls were all instructed to never disclose their last name to anyone. We were also told that if we ever saw any of the girls after we left the home, we were not to acknowledge each other. "After a short length of time," they said, "your lives will be back on track and you will forget about this terrible ordeal."

A social worker provided counseling, but no option other than adoption was ever discussed with me. I was not offered any help or advice about how I might manage to keep my baby. I was not advised of my legal rights, nor told about the possible long-term emotional consequences of relinquishment.

At the home, if a girl openly expressed a desire to keep her baby, she was forced to leave. I remember one girl who decided to keep her baby after it was born. She was not allowed to return to the home—not even to pick up her belongings.

Those of us remaining received a stern lecture about the awful thing she had done by refusing to sign the adoption papers. Her entire family would be disgraced and the child would grow up feeling embarrassed and not as good as other children. We were warned to never discuss her situation among ourselves, or we would be in danger of being expelled from the home.

The girls I met at the maternity home were nothing like what I had expected. They were just regular girls, like me. Most of them had been attending college or working as secretaries before this happened to them. A few were still in high school. The youngest was fifteen and the oldest was twenty-six. There was one black nurse who was being discharged from the Army because she was pregnant. All the others were white middle and upper class girls. They were not promiscuous. Many of them had only the one affair with a boyfriend who made a hasty disappearing act upon learning of the pregnancy.

I still think about one particular girl from the home. She had been engaged to marry her baby's father after he returned from his tour in Vietnam. He never returned. She gave birth to twins and placed them for adoption. She didn't even tell her fiancée's parents that she was pregnant. I think it is so sad that a couple lost their son in that senseless war, and never knew that his twin babies—their grandchildren—were given away to strangers.

When I look back on the birth of my son, I can't believe Mother and Daddy let me go through it completely alone. How could they be so cruel? Even to this day it makes me feel like nobody in the world really cares about me. They never even visited me in the hospital after he was born. I think the personnel from the home told them not to. Maybe if they had seen the baby, they might have encouraged me to keep him.

My labor began late at night. I endured it as long as I could but was very afraid and called the "house mother." She told me to start timing my contractions and wait until they were five minutes apart before bothering her again. She even asked me to try to wait until 8:00 A.M. when the nurses came on duty! I suffered through the rest of the night alone, and at 8:00 A.M. someone called a cab to take me to the hospital.

In the labor room I was left alone in terrible pain. Strange doctors and nurses came in periodically to check my progress but nobody spoke. They just did their jobs. Finally a woman came in to sit with me. She seemed like an angel but I suspect she was a volunteer. Holding my hand, she stayed for the rest of my labor, telling me that "everything will be fine" and "it won't last much longer."

I tried to be brave and never moaned or complained. That woman really made a difference for me. I wish I knew who she was. I'd sure like to thank her.

I don't remember anything about the actual birth because they put me to sleep. When I awoke in the recovery room, the same woman was there. She took my hand and said I'd had a little boy.

"He's fine, dear. He was a little blue, but they gave him oxygen. Everything's okay now."

But it certainly wasn't. After I was taken to my hospital room, I developed a kidney infection and very high fever. I remember that everything seemed rather dream-like. A nurse stuck an IV in my arm and started me on antibiotics. A social worker from the home came by with some papers for me to sign. She said something about temporary custody, but I was too sick to even think. She said this needed to be done right away, so I signed.

After twenty-four hours on the antibiotics I was feeling much better and called for a nurse. I asked to see my baby, but she just hemmed and hawed and wouldn't give me a straight answer. I started crying and making a fuss, demanding that they bring me my baby. Someone finally did, but warned me that I was not allowed to feed him.

I'll never forget those few minutes I spent with my sweet baby. I opened the blanket and examined his perfectly beautiful little body. I counted all his fingers and toes. I told him that I loved him and that I was so sorry that I could not keep him. "I want to do what's best for you, darling, and I have no way of providing for you."

I gave him a name, Jon Steven. Then the nurse came and took him away. It was such a feeling of loss. I cried until I thought my heart would burst.

I was taken back to the home to recover. Five days after delivery they took me to a judge's office to sign the surrender papers. The judge briefly explained the adoption laws and added that I had ninety days in which to change my mind. That was the very first time anyone had suggested that there might be other options.

A little flame of hope lit up inside me. Could I possibly keep my baby? But then I started thinking of the bleakness of my situation. I was eighteen years old with no husband and no job. I didn't want to disgrace my family. I wanted to do what I could to salvage their reputations. I didn't want my baby growing up as an inferior person, and besides, I wanted a husband and family some day. No decent man would have me if I had an illegitimate baby.

The social worker put her hand on my shoulder and said, "You're doing the right thing. Sign the papers."

I did. And the next day someone from the home drove me to the bus station and left me there. Nobody even stayed to make sure I got on the right bus. I felt like they had gotten what they wanted and now they were finished with me.

Daddy picked me up at our town's bus station. He gave me a kiss and drove me home. Nothing was said about my ordeal or the baby. The rest of my family welcomed me home, never guessing the real truth. For everyone except me, life went on as usual. Neither Mother nor Daddy ever mentioned my baby again.

Looking back on it now, I think my parents didn't talk about the baby because they thought it was best for me to forget about it and get on with my life. I had no idea how they really felt, but from then on Daddy always had a very sad look in his eyes. It's hard to describe, but nothing was ever the same between Daddy and me again. It wasn't anger, but more of a deep hurt and disappointment in me, I think.

I used all my energy to try not to think about the baby. I did not discuss it with anyone. I never shared my pain with my friends, my family or anyone. I tried to pretend that there wasn't any baby. But sometimes at night, alone in my room, my feelings would surface and I'd cry into my pillow.

I had always been fairly self-confident and assertive, but I wasn't the same person after that. I felt like whatever it was that made me Bonnie was gone. No matter what I accomplished or achieved, I never felt like it was good enough. I wasn't good enough. I felt dirty, used and useless. I felt like everything I did was fake. I attended college for a while, but dropped out for lack of interest more than anything. I worked halfheartedly at a mindless job.

The following spring, B.J. came back again, wondering if we could possibly work things out. We got married that summer, when my baby was ten months old. I never talked to B.J. about my deep feelings of grief about my baby, but I think he could tell that I was sad. I was actually quite bitter. If the baby had been his, I wouldn't have had to surrender him. B.J. felt sorry for me, I think. He thought that another baby would help, so we started trying.

We had been married barely a year when B.J. was killed in a car accident.

My mother died two months later.

My terrible life just kept getting worse and worse. I was filled with resentment. If B.J. had been my baby's father, I would be a single mother and everybody in the world would rally around me, giving me all kinds of support to raise my child. That's the difference between "orphan" and "bastard" I guess.

I still have a lot of anger about how things were back then. These days, nobody really understands what it was like for me. A person has to live what I lived through to understand it.

I was a complete wreck. I didn't think things would ever get better. One of my aunts had a dear friend whose son had been injured in Vietnam. She came to visit me and commenced to say that it might be a good thing for me to befriend him, since we were both young people who had undergone great tragedies. Among his other injuries, Sam had lost a leg and part of one lung. I started visiting Sam in the hospital, and that's how I met my husband.

We married and had a baby almost right away. Sheila was born the day after our first wedding anniversary. She was so beautiful! I cried because she looked exactly like my first baby. I cried because my mother hadn't lived long enough to see the baby I was going to be allowed to keep. I cried for all the sadness in my world.

In the midst of my sadness, Sheila was a complete joy. I barely let anyone else touch her. I was determined to be a perfect mother and seldom left her with a baby-sitter. When she was just a toddler, Sheila started fantasizing about having a big brother. She used to beg me for a big brother, and it would just tear my heart out.

Another reason for my sadness was my marriage. Things are much better now, but for a time our relationship was quite rocky. I won't go into specifics, but it had to do with Sam's war injuries and subsequent chemical addictions. Anyway, I allowed him to abuse me emotionally. Given my lack of self-esteem at that time, I figured I didn't deserve any better.

But we continued as a family. Sam wanted to have another child. I didn't want any more children. This is strange, but I was afraid that if I had another child it would be a boy and I did not want a boy. I think I was afraid that all the pain would come back if I had a boy.

I sold real estate for a couple of years, then went back to college and got a degree in accounting. When Sheila was nine years old, Sam finally badgered me into having another child. Well, I had a little boy and named him Wayne. And yes, all those memories did come flooding back to me. I held Wayne for almost the entire first three months of his life. I slept in a chair holding him. I thought about my first baby boy all the time, and it started making me a little crazy. I even went to a psychic to try and find out about where he was.

For the next few years I thought and worried about my first baby constantly. I thought about the possibility of searching for him but didn't think I could cope with him rejecting me. So I decided I would never search for him, but would welcome him with open arms if he ever wanted to find me. I wrote a letter to him in care of the Tennessee Human Services. In my letter I told him a little about our family and some medical information. The letter was to be placed in his file. I felt more peaceful after making this final decision about him.

The years went by, and I pursued my career as an auditor. My job, raising the children and coping with Sam's medical needs kept me quite busy. Five years ago Sam had to be put on kidney dialysis, which has been an added strain.

One evening two years ago at dinner time, the phone rang. The voice on the other end said, "Is this Bonnie Keith?"

"Yes." For some reason my heart was pounding.

"I'm from the Tennessee Department of Human Services and I want to inform you about a change in the Tennessee adoption law."

I was speechless, but finally pulled myself together enough to ask her to wait while I went to a more private phone. When I picked up again I asked if this call had something to do with the son I'd placed for adoption.

"Yes," she replied. "And would you be receptive to contact with him?"

"Yes." I told her that my daughter knew of her half brother but Wayne didn't. I was afraid of my first son calling and Wayne answering the phone. I asked if there would be an intermediary, and would she tell me something about him. What is his name?

She refused to tell me anything. She said I would need to write a letter giving permission to release my identity and suggested I rent a post office box if I didn't want him knowing my address at first.

I didn't sleep at all that night. I decided I wasn't going to rent a post office box. After all, this boy was my son. I wouldn't try to hide from him. I sent the letter of release the next day, Express Mail. In my letter I asked that he try to call me on Friday night. I would get the family to leave so we could talk in privacy.

The next few days were very difficult. I kept thinking, "What if he doesn't call? What if he's changed his mind?" I almost drove myself crazy with those kinds of thoughts.

Friday night finally came. I sent Sam and Wayne out to the movies. Sheila was away at college in Alabama. I waited by the telephone. At 8:30 the phone rang. And the most beautiful voice I'd ever heard was on the other end. He sounded so much like my brother, I couldn't believe it! His name was Frank Jeffers and he had lived in Tennessee his whole life. He had been trying to find me since he was eighteen. A former Marine, he had served in the Gulf War. He was married and had a master's degree in accounting. What a coincidence. My degree is in accounting, too.

I could tell that he was well educated, polite and sweet. I loved him immediately. We talked for about two hours. Neither of us could believe how at ease we were with each other. We had so much in common!

I prepared a family photo album for Frank, with pictures of the kids and me and some of when I was a child. I tried to include as many family members as possible. I mailed that to him the following Monday. In turn, he sent me current pictures of him and his wife, Terri, and some pictures of his babyhood and childhood. I was amazed at how much he looked like me. His childhood pictures looked like a male version of me at the same ages.

My daughter and I were in close touch because we were planning her wedding at that time. When I first told Sheila about being in contact with my first son, she was thrilled. The first thing she said was, "Is he a Christian? Can he come to my wedding?"

I had still not told Wayne about his half brother. Sam was very concerned that Wayne would somehow get hurt in all of this and asked me not to. I agreed to put off telling him for a while—just until I could find out if Frank really wanted to have a relationship with us, or if it was just curiosity. I didn't want to put Wayne through any hurt. He was only twelve at the time.

Frank and I talked on the phone frequently for the next couple of weeks. Then we set up a meeting at a South Carolina hotel, located roughly halfway between our home in Georgia and his in Tennessee. Frank and Terri were already there when Sam and I arrived. We went to his room but I didn't even get a chance to knock. He saw me through the window and came out to greet me with a dozen yellow roses.

We hugged each other tightly. This was undoubtedly the happiest moment of my life. The very happiest.

Sam and Terri were very sweet and understanding. They disappeared for the evening, leaving Frank and me alone to talk. I held his hand almost the entire time. I think I made him a little uncomfortable because I was staring at him so much, but I wanted to memorize every detail of his features. I was afraid that I would never see him again. Next morning the four of us went out to breakfast. I think Frank and I both knew by that time that we wanted to have a relationship. This was just too special for just one meeting.

Home again, I went over to Daddy's. "I've got something I need to tell you about regarding my past—a young man. You probably know what I'm about to say."

He knew. "I thought this might happen," Daddy responded.

And then he went on to tell me how the loss of his grandson had affected him. Daddy said, "Not a single day has gone by that I don't think about that baby. I have prayed for him every night."

Daddy has totally accepted Frank as part of the family.

When I told Wayne about his half brother he thought it was a joke. He couldn't believe that his "straight" mother could have something like this in her past. When he realized I was serious, he was shocked, but not angry. Now he and Frank are great buddies. They both love guitars and computers, and Frank is a wonderful role model for him.

Sheila and Frank get along well, and talk on the phone regularly. Although they don't get to see one another very often, she's happy to finally have her big brother.

Sam has been extremely supportive through all this, and shares my happiness about being reunited with my first son.

Frank and I enjoy each other so much. It's like we know each other's hearts. We're so much alike, with similar views and similar ways of reacting. We tell each other everything—even the most private details of our lives. He says, "You're the only person in the world who really understands me."

I feel the same about him. We talk on the phone about once a week and visit via e-mail more often than that. The only problem area is with his family. I've been trying to make friends with his adoptive mom and dad but they seem reluctant. I've written letters thanking them for all they've done and asked to meet them, with lukewarm response.

Frank doesn't want his grandparents to know about me because he's convinced they'd never understand. I don't understand why anybody would be threatened by me. His adoptive mother had him exclusively for twenty-five years and I could never compete with that. I wouldn't want to. I believe that the more people you can love and be loved by, the better.

Frank and Terri have a little boy now—my grandbaby. His name is Sheldon and he's the sweetest little thing. My dearest wish is that some day I can be allowed to be a real grandma to him.

But as it stands right now, I'm kind of a "closet birthmom." I would like things to be different, and maybe everything will work out with time. It bothers me that I still feel so hurt and angry about what happened in my life. I'm hoping that I can eventually put all the anger and bitterness behind me. Somehow, though, I don't think that will ever happen.

Chapter Eleven

Jan

A thousand generations, every one was new—
A thousand generations leading straight to you.
Everyone will tell you that you're just passing through.
Everyone will tell you, everything you do
Sooner or later comes back to haunt you . . .
            (lyrics from the song, "Super-Human")

WE WERE THREE JEWISH GIRLS growing up in a Jewish neighborhood just outside of Detroit, Michigan. Karen, the eldest, was smart and beautiful. Patty, the youngest, had a slight hip deformity, was much protected and much pampered. I was just plain Jan, in the middle, never quite as good as Karen never quite as beloved as Patty.

Father was a pharmacist and Mother had been an elementary school teacher until marriage. Mother was diagnosed with multiple sclerosis before I was born. No one told me what was wrong with her until I was eleven years old. It was much later that I understood that my mother was extremely angry about being cut off in her prime. I've been told that she'd been very active and intelligent—the life of the party. My mother's anger spilled into every part of our family life. My parents had originally planned to have six children. Personally, I'm very glad they didn't.

Since I didn't understand the circumstances of my mother's anger, and since I suffered from what today would probably be called low self-esteem, I just wordlessly assumed that I was bad in some unremarkable way. This I regarded as normal because I never thought anything should be different, or that I deserved better. With a child's incredible ability to accept, I never thought about it at all.

It seemed that other people knew of my mother's illness. When we were attending Patty's graduation from elementary school, one of the teachers introduced us to some other teachers saying, "These are three of the bravest girls I know." My sisters and I were baffled. We never thought of ourselves as brave. We thought of ourselves as undeserving of praise of any kind. We were barely measuring up to what was expected of us, as far as we knew.

Maybe it was because of being brought up in the 1950s, but I was taught that I had no feelings worth mentioning. My confidences to my mother were often exposed and my shortcomings discussed with others. If I felt sad and talked about it, I was told I'd get over it. I began writing poetry in sixth grade (doesn't everybody?) in an effort to try to understand my world.

Karen and I formed a close bond because we both identified our common enemy as Mother. We didn't really connect with Patty, who was four years younger than me and seven years younger than Karen. My mother told Karen and me about menstruation in a matter-of-fact way. I never asked about other related topics. Karen and I compared notes and pieced together the "facts of life" for ourselves.

> My mama told me when I was a child
> "Be careful . . . don't you get too wild—
> 'Cause those who are different—
> They just never fit in . . ."
> (lyrics from the song "Unconventional")

I remember grade school as a cookie-cutter operation, stressing sameness and not rocking the boat. I received fairly decent grades but certainly didn't achieve what I could have. I always loved music and began piano lessons at the age of four. It was later discovered that I have what is called perfect pitch. My musical talents and singing voice earned me some praise by my teachers, rescuing me from the oblivion I might otherwise have experienced.

I felt close to my father but he was mostly absent. Although he didn't discuss finances, I think he had to work long hours to make ends meet, due to the expense of my mother's illness. I loved the few nights a week when he was home. That was when we had real dinners like a real family. The rest of the time everybody ate on the run.

I believe my parents truly loved each other when they got married, but my father couldn't adjust to my mother's illness. He never really dealt with her emotional changes. By illustration, years later, after my mother's death in 1984, my aunt asked at a family gathering, "Was your mother angry?" My sisters and I all said, "Yes," and my dad said, "No," at exactly the same moment. He stood there, staring at us in astonishment.

Being a pharmacist, my father had access to new ideas about treating my mother's disease. One time he tried tranquilizers. She must have liked the effects because she ended up addicted to them. It's hard to say whether she degenerated because of her illness or her addiction. Or maybe it was a combination of the two. After a while, my father started being home less and less. She eventually noticed, and they started fighting often.

Karen and I were teens by then, and even more of my mother's rage was turned on us. Although we were fairly normal, obnoxious teenagers, Mother's reactions were beyond normal. When we complained to Dad, he suggested we "bite our tongues" rather than talk back, which of course made no difference at all. Mother would still rage on.

In 1960 during my thirteenth summer, I got involved with a Zionist Youth Group. This was part of a back-to-Israel movement that was very strong at the time. The leaders of the group convinced my parents to let me go away to camp for two whole weeks. The site was a beautiful state park setting at the top of Lake Michigan's lower peninsula at the meeting of two Great Lakes.

It was the first time I had ever been away from my family. Everything seemed peaceful and fun. I played my guitar and sang for the others—my first real audience. I was heartbroken when camp was over. My mother was afraid I'd get "the Zionist bug" and move to Israel and they'd never see me again. What I did get out of my Zionist adventure was the resolve to get away from Mother at the first possible opportunity, and try to keep peace until then.

In high school I was given some kind of an academic ability test, in which I scored in the ninety-eighth percentile or above in most areas. This resulted in an almost standing appointment with the guidance counselor, who continued to point out to me how I wasn't even close to my potential. I guess it was also standard procedure then to require students like me to meet with a psychologist. At those meetings I was completely uncommunicative. I doubt if I could have articulated how I felt, and my attitude was, "what difference would it make, anyway?"

I was quite shy around my classmates and was self-conscious about my very crooked teeth. I was relieved when my parents finally allowed me to get braces. I really came out of my shell when the braces came off. Until then, my friends were mostly other Jewish girls from the neighborhood. Now I started having friends who were boys. It was intoxicating! I might have even had fun if I had any confidence, but I had no faith in my own feelings and wanted the boys' approval desperately. These were flirty little relationships—nothing serious. But I started feeling like I had found a road to freedom. My mother, as usual, was furious. Our fights became more and more intense.

> . . . I wanna be
> Unconventional—Out of the ordinary—very
> Unconventional—One of a kind
> Unconventional—Totally individual
> Unconventional—One of a kind . . .
> (lyrics from the song "Unconventional")

Around the age of sixteen, I got bored with my circle of friends. All they ever talked about were clothes, boys and makeup. I started being friendly with a more serious and mature group of kids. I had an admirable teacher at that time, too, who began to groom me for college.

My closest friend in school, Linda, encouraged me to take difficult courses and was very supportive. "I know you can do it," she used to tell me.

Linda had been adopted by a Jewish family. We were both raised to believe that Jewish girls always did the right thing. Therefore, sex before marriage was unthinkable, as were babies before marriage. This was in the 1960s, and "getting a reputation" or having a child out of wedlock was considered the absolute worst thing that could happen to a girl. I know how irrational this is now, but we all believed it then.

I remember asking Linda once about her birthmother. "Do you think she was Jewish?"

"Of course not!" Linda retorted. "Jewish girls don't have illegitimate babies!"

After a series of major screaming matches with my parents, my older sister moved away from home. She didn't tell my parents her address or phone number. I was the only one who knew where she was, and I knew that she wasn't telling me everything.

The whole wide world ahead.

It wasn't very long before I heard a rumor that Karen was pregnant. My own sister! I couldn't believe it at first because I admired her so much. But it was true. She made the best of the situation, though, and got married. Eventually, she re-established her relationships with Mother and Dad.

I moved out of my parents' house in January of 1965, three days after my eighteenth birthday. I had a job that paid fifty-five dollars a week and I bought a 1957 Ford for two hundred fifty dollars. I told my parents I wanted to go to a nearby community college. They didn't like any of it but I was eighteen—and free!

I found an apartment for seventy-five dollars a month and rendered it spotless in fifteen minutes flat. That's how small my place was. It was difficult to make ends meet, but I was completely happy.

My girlfriends were green with envy. The guys were very interested—and I was very naive. I had allowed myself to be talked out of my virginity the year before by my then-boyfriend. Horribly guilty about it, I thought I could negate my action by never doing that again. I had definitely been awakened sexually, though, and, as it turned out, my expectations for myself were unrealistic.

One night at the Pizza Palace, I met Jim. He was smooth and good-looking—it was like there was an electric current between us. I was quite smitten with him. He was very intelligent and evidently his parents had plenty of money. It seemed inevitable that we would become sexually involved.

I think having my own apartment fooled me into believing I was ready for all sorts of "adult" behavior. One night our sex was unprotected. The next day, I remember counting the days since my last period on the calendar over and over again. It was exactly fourteen days and I had always been regular. I was filled with dread and, as it turned out, not without cause.

When I became absolutely sure, I told Jim I was pregnant. I said I didn't want to marry him. I didn't want any trouble with his parents or mine, and I wasn't going to ask him for money. I felt angry and what I mostly wanted was for him to go far, far away and let me deal with it. He lived up to my expectations to the letter. He went away without a murmur—except to ask me if I was sure it was his. The nerve.

The last time I had seen him before that conversation was when he fell asleep, drunk, with a cigarette in his hand, and set his mattress on fire. It was pretty clear to me then that he was an alcoholic and had other problems, too. I've never been sorry I didn't marry him.

. . . So how do you know which one it is?
One thing's for sure—it ain't in his kiss.
How do you know? How do you tell them apart?
Until I'm certain, I'll just hold on to my heart . . .
     (lyrics from the song, "Bad Love")

My anger turned into denial, and I kept up that internal fiasco until I got my first case of morning sickness. Reluctantly, I realized I was going to have to make some decisions. I couldn't raise a child on fifty-five dollars a week, and had no prospects of financial security.

Trying to raise a child under my circumstances would be grossly unfair to the child, I reasoned. Although there were rumors in my school of girls who had given up babies, single parents were almost unheard of then. Even divorced mothers were stigmatized—and so were their children. I thought that surely there must be a couple somewhere who could give my baby a decent life. I knew what I had to do, but didn't know how to do it. And I did not want my parents involved. I was very, very frightened inside, but I knew I had to keep my head.

That's what I did for the whole nine months—I completely buried my emotions in order to get through it. Because of our strained relationship, my usual routine was to call my parents only a couple of times a year. Perfect. I moved in with another woman and left no forwarding address, so no one I knew could find me until it was all over. My parents never knew I was pregnant, nor did my younger sister who was only fifteen and couldn't be trusted. Karen was the only member of the family who knew. My older sister was to keep that precious secret for twenty-four years.

I'm still grateful to my friend Linda, who was emotionally supportive to me. I visited her in East Lansing, where she was attending college, as often as I could. She had a boyfriend that her parents were totally opposed to. Our being both in the midst of family rebellions cemented our already close relationship. Linda was the only one of my old friends whom I remained in contact with. She ended up marrying that boyfriend and having five children with him.

Around the middle of my pregnancy, I remember starting to worry about what I was doing with my feelings. "What if I can't get back in?" I thought. "What if I'll never be able to feel emotion again?" But I knew I couldn't afford to spend time worrying about it because being "outside" my emotions was the only way I could survive at that time.

One day when I was walking out of my apartment, a woman who lived down the hall started talking to me. I don't know how she knew, because I wasn't showing yet, but she flat out asked, "Is there a little one on the way?"

After I confirmed her suspicions, she told me about her little daughter, one year old, who was growing up back home in Tennessee, believing her grandmother was her mother.

The woman, Elaine, was in a lot of pain. She recognized the buried pain inside me immediately. In fact, she invited me to live with her rent-free until the baby came. I could pay her back later. Her apartment was just a little larger than mine, but Elaine and I managed well for the next four months.

The people I worked for found out I was pregnant and fired me. The office manager was kind enough to give me the name of a temporary employment agency run by a friend of his. I accepted a position as an office assistant for a bustling ad agency. I went to work every day in multiple girdles and big clothes. Luckily, I didn't show very much, even at eight months.

Perhaps the most ironic thing that happened during my pregnancy was meeting Lee, the man who lived next door to Elaine. We became very close but I wouldn't let him be involved with my pregnancy. In fact, I hid the fact that I was in labor the night my contractions started. Years later Lee and I would marry and separate, but always remain friends.

The hospital in which my child would be born was just across the street. My doctor lived in an apartment upstairs. Elaine helped me find a lawyer who would handle the adoption. This sort of blind luck followed me through my whole pregnancy. Well, they do say that God looks after the children and the fools.

The day before my daughter was born, I woke up knowing I was in labor, even though the doctor had said it would be at least two more weeks. I spend most of the day alone. Elaine came home from work about 6:00 P.M. and Lee stopped by that evening. We stayed up talking until about 11:00 P.M. Every time I had a contraction I left the room. I just didn't want Lee connected to that in any way.

Lee finally left and Elaine and I crossed the street to the hospital. Because I was so small it took some convincing for the nurses believe I was in labor. They admitted me finally and told Elaine to go home. I was alone, worried and scared. I kept my head and kept myself under control.

The baby was born early the next morning. They whisked her away immediately. All I could see was one little blue arm. The doctor assured me that she was fine and healthy. I was relieved but all I could think about was how mad that lawyer was going to be, now that he had to hurry up and find an adoptive couple. I didn't want him to pick someone in a rush.

I had read in some book that if mother/child bonding doesn't take place immediately, it won't happen at all. Letting myself feel some need to bond with my child, I asked Elaine to walk with me to the nursery. The nurses had my baby with her back to the window as if there was something wrong with her. I panicked and asked the nurse to turn her around. She just looked at me and shook her head slowly.

I went back to my room and cried. It was if all the tears I had buried came pouring out. I knew then that there was something terribly wrong with me.

The lawyer visited my hospital room later that day. I guess I looked pretty pathetic. I've always been small in stature and I must have looked like Little Orphan Annie. Anyway, the lawyer said that he felt like he had to help me.

He told me about a nice Jewish couple in New Jersey who had been married a long time and had plenty of money. He said he knew them and trusted them. It sounded all right to me. We told the hospital that I was going to keep my daughter after all, and that they should bring her to me.

By this time the baby's father, Jim, was a distant memory. You can imagine my surprise when I saw my daughter for the first time—and she looked just like him in miniature. I picked her up and held her, working hard to convince myself that I was only baby-sitting, and soon I would give her back to her real mother. "Oh, what a cute baby," I thought to myself. Before I left, I tucked away the little hospital document with her hand and footprints, date and time of birth and the name I gave her, Andrea Ruth Silverberg.

My lawyer flew us to New Jersey, where he acted as my legal guardian. I thought, "I'll just sign the papers and leave." But it wasn't that simple. New Jersey law required an oral statement of intentions before signing relinquishment papers. Furthermore, I was required to not only meet the adoptive parents, but to physically hand Andrea over to them.

I didn't know how I could get through all of that. My stomach was in knots the whole time. The couple seemed years older than I was and very respectable. I gave them my daughter and flew back to Michigan alone.

Back at the apartment, my grief exploded in gut-wrenching sobs. I've never cried so hard in my life and I've never been so bereaved. Even thinking about it now, I still feel the shadow of that awful aching loss. Knowing I did the right thing was absolutely no consolation.

> . . . And the world turns 'round, and the rivers roll,
> And I feel you in my body and in my soul.
> No matter what I say,
> No matter what I do—
> I know I'll never be free of you . . .
> (lyrics from the song "Just Can't Leave Your Love")

Almost right away, I went to work for the temporary agency again, wanting to get out on my own and pay Elaine back. Lee and I started getting romantically involved. He was very sweet to me, and I knew I could trust him because he's seen me at my worst and still wanted me. We were both pretty young—I was twenty and he was almost twenty-one.

Aside from my feelings about Lee, I was pretty numb emotionally, although I didn't realize it at the time. I had no real direction. I thought vaguely about getting married, having children and just sinking into some kind of oblivion.

One afternoon the lawyer called to tell me it was time to file the adoption papers. During our meeting I looked across his desk and read my daughter's new name upside down. It had been changed from the name I gave her, but the adoptive couple used the first name, Andrea, that I had given her as the middle name. I was very touched by that. I signed the papers and walked home in a kind of haze.

Lee's job required that he move to New York City. I moved there too, and we got married after about a year. I still wasn't thinking much about the future, except that maybe I could have a child soon, to make up for the daughter I couldn't raise.

Wondering about Andrea's whereabouts, I called information and asked for the town in New Jersey where I knew the parents lived. The operator gave me the number, but I never called. I did, however, call information often enough to know the adoptive family lived there for three more years. Then, one day I called and they were no longer listed.

Lee and I began growing away from each other at an incredible pace. Both of us hated our marriage, even though we still liked one another. We agreed to part but we didn't want the stigma of being divorced. According to New York law if both parties had agreed to have children and one party reneged, the marriage could be annulled. Truth is, I just didn't get pregnant. But that was a good way to end our marriage.

After a brief affair with a law student, I began feeling so rejected I lost interest in everything. I developed an eating disorder and gained thirty pounds in one month. I remember telling Karen, my sister, that I thought I must not deserve anything good, after what I had done. She did her best to convince me otherwise, but she was having her own problems at that time. Her husband was physically abusive to her and chased after other women. As much as I loved her it was hard for me to believe that either one of us deserved better.

> . . . Bad love will abandon you and then you're better off.
> Bad love is worse than no love at all,
> Bad love is worse than no love at all . . .
> (lyrics from the song "Bad Love")

I left New York in 1971 when I was twenty-four, in an attempt to get away from everything. I dusted off my musical skills, became my own version of a hippie and was anxious to travel. I had overcome my eating disorder and pulled myself together once again. I had an idea of going to California to perform. I stopped in Austin, Texas, on the way.

I got a job, entered college and got a BA in music and another in anthropology from the University of Texas. I became serious about my career as a singer/songwriter around this time. I performed in Nashville for six months, then in Los Angeles for about five years, achieving some success along the way. I always returned to Austin, though.

By the time I was thirty, I despaired of ever having a committed relationship or children. I started seeing John, who attended virtually all of my shows in the Austin area. I knew it would not last but my biological clock was definitely ticking. I allowed myself to become pregnant, knowing that I would be raising this child alone.

Raina, my second daughter, was born in 1979. I was joyful and felt like my whole life had been leading up to her birth. I was so grateful to be able to bring her home.

I had always saved my first daughter's hospital document. Cradling Raina in my arms, I held the document in front of her and said, "Raina, this is your sister." A friend came to visit just then. She found me with Raina on one arm, the document in the other hand and crying.

Another friend of mine, who knew others who had lost children the way I lost Andrea, started an informal support group at that time. I didn't know it then, but that was the beginning of Austin's most active adoptive search organization.

Throughout all of this, I never told my family about my first daughter. My older sister and I stopped talking about it, and anyone would think I had forgotten about it. But every year on Andrea's birthday I would wonder where she was, and especially if she was still alive. I couldn't stand the anxiety of thinking about it very long. One year on her birthday I dated everything the next day, and didn't realize until later what I had done.

Sometimes when I held Raina's hand and the hand of one of her friends I would think, "This is what it is like to have two daughters."

Once I went to the library to learn how to search for Andrea. I sent a letter to an organization in Michigan and another to New Jersey, explaining the particulars of my first daughter's birth. Michigan sent back a questionnaire, which I completed, but I never heard from New Jersey. In the end I didn't do anything else because I didn't think I had the right to search.

I married Jimmy in 1983 when Raina was four. What a mistake! It didn't take me long to discover that he was abusive. He also molested my little daughter. I divorced him immediately. I have never seen him again.

> . . . But when you look in the mirror
> I know what you see.
> You see yourself waiting
> To be set free . . .
> (lyrics from "Super-Human")

Knowing there were "demons" lurking within me, I began seeing a therapist. I learned that I needed to stop damaging myself and could not risk damaging Raina any further. I spent the next two years without men, concentrating on my relationship with Raina. Although I told my therapist about Andrea, I never told Raina about her sister because I didn't want to burden her with my grief and unanswered questions.

When my mother died in 1984, I worked through some of my issues with the therapist, but many of them still remain unresolved.

In 1987 I won a regional song-writing contest, which resulted in my attending a class entitled, "How to Make a Record." Andy, the owner of a small production company, was teaching the class. Interestingly, we traveled in the same circles, but somehow had never met. Andy ended up producing my first album—and a whole lot more. He's still my producer/engineer, as well as my beloved. They say third time's a charm, and it certainly has been for me.

Andy is a wonderful person who also had much to heal from. When we met he was recovering from a nasty custody battle over his daughter, Melody. He asked me, "Do you think a person can ever really recover?"

I told him about my first daughter then, and said, "No, I don't think we recover, exactly, but we learn to go on."

> . . . I know it isn't easy to smile,
> When nothing goes the way that you plan.
> But baby, we've got love enough to last quite awhile,
> So if there's rocky roads ahead
> We can walk them hand in hand . . .
> (lyrics from the song "Years in the Future")

We married two years later. The wedding took place just after Raina's bat mitzvah, and my dad and sisters came to Austin for that occasion. It was a full house, but everybody got along, thankfully.

One month after my marriage to Andy, on Christmas Eve, my younger sister, Patty, called. She said, "Jan, a woman called here for you . . ."

Immediately, I knew. Andy walked into the room at that exact moment and I blurted out, "My daughter's looking for me!"

I heard Patty gasp, "It's true, then?" but the lump in my throat was too big for me to answer her.

I finally told her it was. She said that some "search volunteer" had called, and then had put Robyn (Andrea) on the phone. Patty didn't know whether she was really my daughter or what my response would be.

"I have been waiting for twenty-four years for this moment," I told Patty. Then I apologized for never telling her. Patty told me that Robyn's adoptive mother had died seven years before, and her Aunt Suzy had put an inquiry on the Internet, after finding the hospital bill in the mother's safety deposit box with my name and Michigan address on it. The search volunteer saw the inquiry and called Robyn, offering to help her find me.

Despite all the bouncing around the country I had done, it took my first daughter only four days to find me. My sister gave me Robyn's phone number in New York. It was more than an hour before I could decide what to say.

"Robyn? This is Jan," was what I finally said. I was so nervous I could barely talk. I could tell she was nervous, too. I told Robyn that I had hoped to hear from her when she was eighteen, and then when that didn't happen, I thought maybe at twenty-one, but that didn't happen, either. I told her that I didn't think I should search because I didn't want to disrupt her life. Also, that I wouldn't have been able to stand it if I'd found out she was dead.

She said that her adoptive mother and father had divorced when she was eleven and that she had been so angry that she ended up in therapy. It was the therapist who told her, without permission, that she was adopted. She became estranged from both her adoptive parents. The mother died when Robyn was nineteen and she felt too guilty to search for me then, because of the negative relationships with her parents. She felt it would be disloyal to them.

She made one earlier attempt to find me but her adoptive dad mistakenly told her that her middle name had been my first name. Of course, this was before they found the hospital bill in the safety deposit box. If her adoptive mother hadn't died she might never had found me. You see, the mother had not even wanted Robyn to know she was adopted!

It wasn't until after Robyn's marriage and the birth of her son, Casey, that she decided there were too many unanswered questions in her life. That was when she asked her Aunt Suzy to inquire on the Internet.

I called my home number after completing that first conversation with Robyn. My father answered the phone. He said, "I've been told. Is it true?"

"Yes."

There was a long pause. "So what does this mean?"

I knew that if I didn't make him laugh, at least one of us would have a stroke. "Well," I replied, "for one thing it means you're a great-grampa. I bet you thought you were just a good one!"

It worked, thank goodness. Dad has been wonderful ever since. He even set up a trust fund for my little grandson, Casey. The only reference Dad ever made to my secret pregnancy was that he understood the circumstances but was sad that I had to go through all of that alone.

Robyn and I wrote letters back and forth, sent pictures and made hundreds of long distance phone calls until the following April when we finally met in person, and I was finally able to hug her and my five month-old grandson. I can't even describe those incredible feelings. She was so beautiful. And that sweet baby. Robyn's husband Jim was in the army, so that meeting took place later.

. . . You look like an angel, you look like an angel—
And all the time between . . . gone!
Just like a dream,
For dreams are like the wind . . .
(lyrics from the song "Angel")

We had a little "coming out" party for Robyn. My dad came to Austin to meet her, and they hit it off right away. My sisters welcomed her warmly. Raina was ecstatic to find out that she had an older sister. In fact, she laughed out loud when I told her.

"It sounds more like a soap opera than real life," she said.

The only person who seemed negative was Robyn's adoptive grandmother, who is even now apparently afraid that I'm going to "steal" Robyn away from them. My first daughter, however, has an enormous heart, and no one is in danger of losing her.

As it turned out, Robyn needed some adjustment time. My marriage, followed quickly by a new sister, brother-in-law and nephew was a little much to take at first. But Raina and Robyn are becoming good friends.

When Robyn and Jim had their second son, Josh, I went out to New York for a week, to help and attend the bris along with most of her family. Everyone was very cordial, and treated me like a distant relative, which is how I view them. Robyn introduced me to some of her friends as her "mom." I looked around quickly to see if that offended anyone. If it did, I never knew.

At one point, Robyn told me that she feels sorry for her brother and sister because she has a mom and they don't. I told her to let them know they are welcome at my house anytime. Her brother e-mails messages to me regularly and we all exchange cards and letters.

From what Robyn told me, it's obvious that things would have been different if her adoptive mother had lived. Her Aunt Suzy confirms this and said that her mother would have been opposed to her finding me. Perhaps her mother and I might have gotten past the negative feelings, or perhaps not. I don't think our reunion would have gone as smoothly if my mother had been alive, either. Robyn and I have talked about our similar issues and feelings about our mothers. I think Robyn is closer to resolving her problems than I am. But we help each other.

I once hesitantly admitted to her that I was afraid I had profited at someone else's expense. She answered, "I think that wherever our respective mothers are now, they understand." I take this as evidence of what a special person Robyn is.

So much has changed since the reunion. I had always discounted my younger sister, Patty, as someone not worth knowing, but I found out that she is a delightful human being. Despite living far apart, we three sisters are closer than we've ever been.

I knew my dad, in his own way, had been trying to make amends since my mother's death. I had mostly ignored these attempts, but after meeting Robyn, I was somehow able to let my anger go. All the barriers dropped away. I found myself more willing to understand Dad's point of view after I gave up the secrets. He's been a champ, too, immediately making a place in his heart for Robyn and her family.

Andy and Robyn's husband, Jim, have gone fishing together and get along just fine. Andy was very supportive to me all through the upheavals that Robyn's return brought forth. All that sudden surfacing of old memories! He was unbelievably tolerant through it all.

Our lives are as settled as they'll ever be, probably. Melody, Andy's daughter, lives mostly with us now. She's almost nine years old, loves animals and has beautiful Mexican-American features like her mother. Raina is facing some fairly normal growing up challenges, but we're being consistent with our "tough love," and I know life will work out for her.

My musical career is going smoothly. The newness of my first daughter has worn off, but not the delight, relief and gratitude. I never realized how wounded I was until the wound was healed. I thank the universe for returning my daughter to me.

I know that we have been very fortunate. There were lots of other possible outcomes. Nevertheless, even if our relationships had not turned out so well, I believe that the universe was out of balance while we were kept away from one another.

I regret that I couldn't raise Robyn and couldn't know her. I couldn't know if she had what she needed, or even if she was alive. This still seems wrong to me. I used to have nightmares about the terrible things that could have happened to her. I was never sure if I hadn't just "thrown her to the wolves."

One might relinquish one's rights to parenthood, but one never really relinquishes the child. The universe is back in balance now.

* * *

Fourteen-years later . . .

A SURPRISING AMOUNT OF TIME has passed since Robyn and I were reunited. Our relationship has settled into a warm closeness. At the beginning, we were so excited, almost frantic, about making up for lost time and getting to know each other. I remember being devastated the first time we disagreed about something. All of that has smoothed out now and we are no longer so emotional about our interactions.

I adore her. She's a generous and thoughtful person. And she's been through a lot over the years. At the end of my original story, Robyn had two sons and was married to Jim, who was in the Army. For many reasons, the marriage didn't last. For one thing, she found out he was asking *Robyn's family in Florida.*

to be deployed. Apparently, he was supposed to talk to her before volunteering, but he had never done that, nor did he mention that his deployment was voluntary. They tried to get back together after an initial separation, and the result was her third son, Brandon. But they still couldn't make it work. So Jim left, and Robyn moved to Florida, where her adoptive dad lived. He had offered to help her get settled. His help turned out to be minimal at best, but she'd always wanted to live in Florida. She is happy there and has made a life for herself.

Robyn has a wonderful new man in her life. John refers to the boys as "our kids" and takes very good care of Robyn. They've been together now for about five years, and have been engaged for about two. They are buying a nice house and are very happy together.

As for Andy and me, we get to be the grandparents of three fine boys. We get to be the ones who send the coolest birthday and Christmukah (as Robyn calls it) presents. Casey, the oldest, recently graduated from high school and is headed for college. Josh, the fiery redhead in the middle, is an A student and plays lacrosse. Brandon, the youngest, is into action figures, very imaginative and about to be Bar Mitzvah.

For a while I had mixed feelings about being a grandma. It seemed like a bit of a shock. I remember one particular visit to Florida. I played a house concert near enough for Robyn and John and the boys to come. They were a little bit late and I was already on stage when they arrived. Nevertheless, Josh, who was about ten years then, shouted out "Hey, Grandma Jan!" My first thought was, "Well, my cover's blown, isn't it!" But they're such great kids, each in their own way. I got used to the title.

> . . . She made me a granny before my time.
> How can that be when I'm in my prime?
> My knees still bend and I can see just fine.
> She made me a granny before my time! . . .
> (lyrics to the song "Granny Song")

Robyn is the perfect mom for three boys to have. She has a rough-and-tumble attitude, and is really good at keeping them in line. I admire her parenting skills a great deal.

Melody, Raina, Robyn and Jan.

For about the past ten years, we've been visiting Florida every December. Raina and Melody used to come along but now they're all grown up with their own lives. The girls do continue their sisterly relationships on the phone and on Facebook.

Most of Robyn's adoptive family and her birth family have met. My older sister, Karen, the only one in my family who knew of Robyn's existence for all those years, has finally met her. They were very impressed with one another. Raina has met Lisa, Robyn's older sister from her adoptive family, but not Robyn's brother. Raina currently lives in New York City, where she works as a publicist. One year, I gave a performance in New York on Robyn's birthday. Lisa and her husband, Rob, came to the performance. Raina and about twenty of her friends were there, too. During the performance, I telephoned Robyn and held up the phone so everyone in the room could sing "Happy Birthday". Lisa captured the event on video.

Robyn told me once that before we actually met face to face, she had thought about how nice it was that she was bringing me a baby (Casey) to make up for not being able to be the mom who raised her. I was so touched. I told her that I love the boys very much, but for me, she is the prize. Getting to be her mom now is a blessing far beyond any I could have hoped for.

When Melody, Andy's daughter by his previous wife came to live with us, I wasn't surprised, given her background, that she would be a child with issues. Her mother had pretty much let her run the show. No wonder Melody had a hard time with discipline and order in her life.

The most challenging times for Andy and me were shepherding Raina through adolescence. Being the child of a single parent can't be easy, and she had been through a number of huge life changes authored by me, mostly. Raina became a "troubled teen" and it was more work than I thought I was capable of. I truly wasn't sure either one of us would survive it. There were drug issues, truancy, questionable company and even a trip to juvenile detention. With the help of "Tough Love," we all made it through.

When life started settling down, I began pursuing my music again, which I'd abandoned when all of that chaos sapped my energy. I remember announcing to my Tough Love support group, "My small step this week is to take my life back." Then I invited them all to the performance I had booked for that weekend.

Since then I've put out two more albums, the second of which is songs that were inspired by all these experiences. Payback, in other words. I'm currently working on a new album. My recordings have won awards and gotten radio airplay. I've done performances all over the country and in Europe. I believe songwriting has saved my sanity. I use it as a sort of journal—a road to a better perspective and a way to work through my feelings. The work of making a song out of the mixed bag of my life makes me filled and fulfilled. The end of my original story is the end of this story, too. The universe is back in balance now.

> . . . But everyone fulfills their perfect destiny
> Whether by fate or faith or chance.
> The snowflakes pirouette into the icy trees
> And the stars revolve in their stately dance.
>
> And the time keeps passing
> And life keeps happening
> And after all
> We are only human
> After all
> We're all only human.
>   (lyrics to the song "Only Human")

Top Ten Ways to Help Ensure a Happy Reunion and Relationship

PRACTICAL ADVICE FOR REUNITING FAMILIES

1. **BE YOURSELF**. (Am I too fat? Will she think I'm dumb? Will they think I have bad intentions?) You are who you are and it's best not to worry about it. Know that you're a good person, be honest with yourself and others, and above all, try to relax.

2. **BE RESOURCEFUL**. (What should I expect? What if he hates me? I'm feeling afraid about what might happen.) You may feel more in control of the possibilities by finding out how other families have handled reunions. In addition to my book, there is much information in the library and the Internet. It might be a good idea to seek out the advice of a professional counselor, too.

3. **BE RESPECTFUL**. (Why can't we all spend Christmas together? We should be together on her birthday.) Your newfound relatives have an entire history—which doesn't include you. It is important to respect their lifestyles and desires, just as they need to respect yours.

4. **BE SENSITIVE**. (Separated all these years—let's make up for lost time! I want to have lunch once a week!) Be a good listener, and try to be aware of how others are feeling. In the joy and uncertainty of getting to know one another, we need to remember that it's normal for adoptive parents to feel threatened or at least unsure about how to react. When I met my son, I wrote many letters to his parents. Those letters helped reassure them that they weren't going to lose their son. Keep in mind that adopted people are fiercely loyal to their adoptive parents, too.

5. **BE PATIENT**. (I've known her for three weeks and she's never even hugged me.) Sometimes it takes years for people to bond. And

sometimes people end up slowly drifting away from each other. Be patient with your relationship. Don't try to push, and don't hang back needlessly. Let things develop naturally. I've been reunited with my adult son since 1986 and we're still getting to know each other.

6. **TALK ABOUT IT**. (I wonder if he thinks I didn't want him. I wonder if she knows that I love her. I wonder if I should tell him the truth about his conception. I wonder if I should tell her that I prayed for her every night.) Don't try to second-guess anyone. The best way to find out what you want to know is to ask. Use your intuition. Be open and honest.

7. **BE UNDERSTANDING**. (Why are they acting this way? I would never act this way.) You may feel a bit like an emotional octopus - trying to understand everybody all at once. Don't forget, siblings, grandparents, everybody's relatives, friends and co-workers are all going to be influenced—in different ways—by your reunion.

8. **ASK FOR HELP**. (I can't handle this! It's more difficult than I thought it would be.) The most courageous people I know are those who see a counselor or other mental health professional when things get rough. You don't have to be in this alone. Trusted friends are good sounding boards, too.

9. **KEEP IT IN PERSPECTIVE**. (This is only part of who I am. I have many other things in my life, even though right now this feels like the only thing.) Especially at first, it's easy to make your reunion a central focus. Don't forget the other people and activities in your life. And rest assured, things will calm down with time.

10. **ENJOY YOUR LIFE**. (All in all, the world is a wonderful place, when we stop to think about it.) No matter how your reunion and relationships turn out, remember that you're in charge of your own happiness. You can't control the behavior of other people. What you do with your life is ultimately up to you.

Some Questions Adoptive Parents Ask Birthmothers

After my book, *Shadow Mothers: Stories of Adoption and Reunion* was published, I was invited to be a speaker for an adoption support and education group in Silver Spring, Maryland. The director gave my talk the title, "The Second Most Important Thing About Adoption." In the publicity materials she wrote, "The most important thing about adoption is that it creates our families . . . the second most important thing about adoption is that our children have birthparents and, regardless of the degree of contact or knowledge we have about them, those birthparents have great meaning for our children." The goal of the event was to invite adoptive parents to examine openly and honestly the issue of birthparents. They were to have a real live birthparent as their guide—me.

I didn't know what to expect. Would they fear me? Shun me? Hate me? Would I be a target for rotten tomatoes tossed from the back of the room? I had been told that some of the parents might be there just to see what a real birthmother looked like. I thought that the fact that I am also an adoptive mom might make me a little easier to accept.

That morning I combed my hair carefully to make sure neither of my horns were showing. My dear husband walked me to the Metro station in D.C. and put me on the train that would deliver me to Silver Spring. I felt strangely calm and confident. I knew most of what I wanted to say and decided to just go with it.

Nearly seventy people were crowded into the room and more chairs kept being hauled out of the closet. I began by telling them that I wrote my book to promote understanding of birthparents, because understanding is the cornerstone to building relationships between people. I said a few words about Tom—how we had met twelve years earlier—how it had been for me to live in a closed adoption, not knowing if he were alive or dead. I talked about how I could never forget about him, even though that's what society expected of me. I looked up from my papers and saw tears in the eyes of several women in the front row.

I read a few excerpts from my book. More tears. I read some of my poems and then said, "Especially when I was a single parent, I tried to get as much love and positive input as possible for my children. There's no reason, other than the barriers we ourselves build, why a child can't have more than one type of parent." I talked about adopting my daughter, my feelings about her birthmother, the nebulous nature of adoption, how to prepare for the future as a secure parent raising a secure child, how open adoption is evolving and how we as parents are helping write the history of adoption.

There were many questions and comments. Here are just a few of the issues that were raised that day. To clarify, adoptive mother is referred to as Amom, adoptive father as Adad, birthmother as Bmom, birthfather as Bdad. Somehow, those terms feel fair and correct to me.

Amom:
> My child's Bmom abandoned her and didn't seem to love her at all. What shall I tell my daughter when she asks if her birthmother loved her?

Me:
> This is just my opinion, but I can't imagine carrying a child for nine months, giving birth to her and placing her for adoption without love. Of course she loved her.

Amom:
> Really?

Me:
> Of course.

Amom.
> Oh, thank you for telling me this. (tears.)

Adad:
> I have a picture of my eleven-year-old son's Bmom. When should I show it to him?

Me: The picture does belong to him, but as his parent and role model, only you can decide when he's ready for the picture. I'd suggest talking openly with him, as it sounds like you have, and maybe let him decide when he's ready to see a photo. In this way you are showing him your respect, and earning his at the same time.

Amom: My child doesn't seem to care about the topic of his birthparents. What should we do about it?

Me: Even though he doesn't talk about it, you can bet he thinks about it. Maybe not all the time, but sometimes. My daughter never seemed interested in the subject until she graduated from college. Every child is different. Let him set the pace and let him know that you are supportive and not threatened by the subject.

Amom: My child's adoption is semi-open. I think his Bmom would like to have it more open, but I don't know if I can deal with that. Won't it make him confused?

Me: Although I'm not an expert on open adoption (and who is—it's all relatively new), research indicates that parents who have some form of contact with their children's Bparents are often better able to trust and overcome their fears. Kids are resilient. They tend to handle situations as well as their parents are handling things. That's why it's so important for you to become as secure as possible with your roles as parents. Self confident parents raise self confident children.

Adad: Our child's Bmom and Bdad are really bad people. they have all sorts of drug and alcohol problems and have been in trouble with the law. Our adoption is closed. What shall we tell our child about his Bparents?

Me: First of all, you don't know they are bad people. You don't really know the reasons or experiences that led them down that sad road. I think you can definitely give them the benefit of the doubt. If it were my child, I'd tell her that her Bmom and Bdad had a lot of problems and they knew they wouldn't be good parents. Of course, it's up to you to gauge the readiness of your child for each level of information. I believe in telling the truth, but all the details aren't always necessary.

So many issues were raised that day, I think we could have continued into the night. After the session ended, some people shook my hand and others hugged me. Looking back on the experience, I know that I received a lot more than I gave from this group of thoughtful parents. That sunny day, in that Maryland schoolroom, some important work was accomplished. A deeper understanding took root in our lives. This understanding will flourish and blossom into the lives of our children. Call us Aparents or Bparents—but we are all on the same side. We persevere for the sake of the children. For the love of the children.

Out of the Shadows

What were the things that you found surprising in these stories?

Did you find any similarities in the stories? If so, what were they?

Is there anyone in your life who has been touched by adoption? Was there a secret involved?

If you think the author presented the stories in an interesting and sensitive way, how do you think she achieved this?

Do you think the author gave consideration to all sides of the adoption triad? Do you think she showed different opinions fairly or correctly? Do you think she seemed to have a bias? If so, why?

Since these mothers all signed "Agreements of Relinquishment," which was basically a promise to cut all ties with the child, do you think it is right for the mother to come back into her child's life?

What factors, in your opinion, affect the success or failure of an adoption reunion?

In an adoption reunion, what do you think would be the "proper" role of the birth parents? The adoptive parents? The adoptee?

How would you feel if you, for any reason, felt forced to place your child for adoption? How would you proceed with your life?

How do you think you would feel as an adoptive parent if a birthparent came into the picture?

How has society changed since these "Shadow Mothers" gave birth to the children they placed for adoption?

What role does open adoption play in society? Do you think people are better adjusted and live happier lives in an open adoption?

How has this book affected your ideas about adoption and reunion? Will it have any affect on your life, opinions or actions?

About the Author

Linda Back McKay is a poet, writer, coach and teaching artist. She teaches classes at the Loft Literary Center in Minneapolis, MN and edits poetry and prose manuscripts for individual clients. Her work has appeared in literary publications such as *Great River Review, Water-Stone Review, White Pelican Review, To Sing Along the Way* and *33 Minnesota Poets.* She is recipient of several awards and residency fellowships from the Anderson Center for Interdisciplinary Studies and Norcroft. McKay is author of the groundbreaking nonfiction work, *Shadow Mothers: Stories of Adoption and Reunion* (North Star Press.) That book was inspiration for the play *Watermelon Hill,* which was produced by the History Theatre in St. Paul, MN. Her poetry collections include *The Cockeyed Precision of Time* (White Space Press) and *The Next Best Thing* (Nodin Press.) She lives by the Mississippi River with David McKay and a fast red Harley-Davidson motorcycle. McKay's next book will be a "motorcycle memoir. Visit www.lindabackmckay.com